Playwriting and Young Audiences

Playwriting and Young Audiences
Collected Wisdom and Practical
Advice from the Field

Matt Omasta and Nicole B. Adkins

intellect Bristol, UK / Chicago, USA

First published in the UK in 2017 by
Intellect, The Mill, Parnall Road, Fishponds, Bristol, BS16 3JG, UK

First published in the USA in 2017 by
Intellect, The University of Chicago Press, 1427 E. 60th Street,
Chicago, IL 60637, USA

A catalogue record for this book is available from the
British Library.

Copy-editor: MPS Technologies
Production Manager: Richard Kerr
Cover designer: Emily Dann
Typesetting: Contentra Technologies

Print ISBN: 978-1-78320-748-0
ePDF ISBN: 978-1-78320-749-7
ePUB ISBN: 978-1-78320-750-3

Printed and bound by TJ International Ltd, Padstow, Cornwall

To all my mentors, especially Johnny Saldaña.
-Matt Omasta

To Eric, Zoe, and Isaac, with gratitude for the daily inspiration.
Also, to my mom, my most enduring champion.
-Nicole B. Adkins

Contents

Foreword

Suzan Zeder

The generosity of "and"

We dwell in our conjunctions and depend upon our prepositions. Although the subject and verb in most sentences get the most attention, it is the humble conjunction that provides the connective tissue between one thing and another, one thought and another, one being and another, as it falls to the preposition to define the nature of the relationship between them. It is, therefore, appropriate that the first part of the title of this book is *Playwriting AND Young Audiences*; the operant word being "*and*." In the three little letters of that conjunction are held all of the prepositions that describe the diverse dimensions of the work we do creating theatre for, about, by, to, and with young people. The myriad manifestations of the field include professional productions of plays for young and family audiences, plays with child protagonists, contemporary original plays, a plethora of adaptations of familiar fairy tales and fables and works of contemporary literature, devised work that promotes social change and encourages activism, *and* an abundance of programs that directly involve young people in schools and community settings. The field of Theatre for Young Audiences (TYA) ranges wide and deep, even though it has existed in the United States for scarcely a century.

In interviews with no less than 75 artists and practitioners, Matt Omasta and Nicole Adkins have collected wisdom and practical advice that goes far beyond simply providing assistance to the would-be playwright who wishes to know what this thing called TYA is all about. In this book they provide a deeply moving account of the state of the art and the pulse of the practice. They capture the thoughts, experiences, intentions, and aspirations of playwrights, directors, designers, dramaturgs, scholars, and educators who have devoted their professional lives and their artistic endeavors to work that celebrates the dignity and depth of young people. Together with their own review of the critical and descriptive literature of the field, Omasta and Adkins synthesize a wealth of information into a cohesive whole. This is more than a "how to" book, it is a "what I did" and "why I did it" and "what you might do" compendium that combines mechanics and aesthetics and philosophy and practicality.

In these pages you will hear from icons of the field – *and* current Artistic Directors of major companies – *and* educators and scholars heading the most prestigious university programs in the country – *and* heads of the primary programs in new play development. *and*, of course, you will hear from playwrights, established and emerging, writers who have defined the canon of TYA dramatic literature – *and* writers at the very beginning of the ascendant arcs of their writing lives. Building on a foundation of advice from established leaders are the younger voices, the new guard, who are re-making the field in their own image.

What is particularly impressive is the variety of points of view from working professionals from all parts of the country and all stages of their careers who provide testimony to the promise and the pitfalls involved in all phases of creating new work for young audiences. From a lucid discussion of different definitions of childhood, the marginalization of children in our society, and what constitutes a TYA play; to a fascinating analysis of genre, style, and form; to a thought-provoking exploration of ethical issues such as the role of ideology, values, and often conflicting cultural norms, this book provides no easy answers, no pat solutions, no single dogma. *And* that is exactly its value. It will be up to the playwrights, producers, directors, and dramaturgs reading this book to formulate their own philosophies and personal ethics, but they will have plenty of support from the kindred spirits represented here.

With so many different points of view and so many topics explored, one might think the result would be a patchwork. But quite is opposite is true; Omasta and Adkins have wisely avoided stitching together a pastiche of single sentences and partial philosophies. The quotes in this book are long, meaty, and muscular. In them you will hear the voices of the speakers in whole stories, reasoned opinions, and detailed explanations. Because the book returns time and again to the same speakers in different chapters, you will come to know them as individuals. You will almost feel like they are speaking directly to you one on one. The book wraps around you like a quilt, rather than hanging from your shoulders like a loosely woven fabric.

The overall sequencing of information is also canny. Moving from overall definitions and discussions of the field in general, the chapters unfold much in the same way as the creative process of writing a play. First with finding a subject, creating the world of the play, finding voice for characters – particularly for young characters – then to building a plot and creating that first full draft. The book goes on to explore a variety of approaches to new play development and provides valuable references to specific programs where new work is nurtured and given support through workshops and reading. Both the positive and challenging aspects of new play development are presented, as some plays are literally "developed to death" never finding the fulfillment in full production that they need to complete their developmental journey. The book does not shy away from the difficulties faced, particularly by emerging artists, in getting their work produced. Speakers give free voice to their fears and frustrations as well as their joys, dreams, and fondest hopes for the life of their art and their own lives as artists.

Most sobering is the frank and unintentionally ironic chapter titled *Income Potential*. The straight unvarnished truth from every speaker is that most, if not all playwrights, old or young, established or emerging, will never make a living solely by writing plays for young audiences. Financial remuneration of writers working in "adult" theatre is not much better, but it is less parsimonious than royalties and commissions and earning potential in TYA. But the chapter goes on to explore "complimentary careers" such as teaching and a variety of day jobs. It also provides useful information about grants, fellowships, and residency programs that can help keep the wolf from the door. A darker truth is that even the best-known, most prolific, most highly revered playwrights in the field will never receive the kind of fame, name recognition, artistic visibility, and respect that their counterparts in the "adult" theatre may be lucky enough to achieve. There are no Tonys in TYA, except through our own professional organizations. To the general public and to the larger artistic community, we need to be twice as good to be taken half as seriously.

But the collective voices in this book reveal something more abiding than momentary fame or fortune. Stripped of any illusions about glory or profit, the book speaks ... no, sings ... of a different kind of calling, a deeper purpose, a kind of indigenous optimism that echoes in every voice in this book. Because the marrow of the work has to do with children as both subjects and recipients, there is a kind of altruism that eschews irony and despair, that is born of hope and a commitment to social justice, that demands that artists and practitioners bring their *best* game to the table.

As educator Tamara Goldbogen states, "I love the idea of creating what might be the first theatre piece that a young person experiences." Playwright Barry Kornhauser claims, "it is ... a sacred trust." Artistic Director Janet Stanford concludes, "As TYA artists, we have the privilege of making stories – old and new – that become a young person's reference point – their source of strength and inspiration – forever."

and ... it doesn't get better than that!

Acknowledgments

We are deeply grateful to everyone who played a role in bringing this book to fruition. In particular, we would like to thank Suzan Zeder for her thoughtful insights into the book and for composing its foreword.

Thanks to Kathy Kryzs and Arizona State University Library's Child Drama Collection for access to a wealth of information about the history of our field.

We thank student research assistants Sarah Butterfield, Kimberly Lamping, and Kaitlin Terry for their work sorting through copious articles and identifying salient information. Thanks to Kenya Thompson for her assistance in compiling the index.

This book would not have been possible without our peer reviewers and dedicated collaborators at Intellect: Amy Damutz, Jessica Mitchell, Richard Kerr and Tim Mitchell.

Finally, we are extremely grateful to each of the artists and scholars who contributed their voices to this project and who are named in the Notes on Contributors section at the end of this book; their insights are at the core of this text.

Preface

Generations of young people have enjoyed attending theatrical performances in professional theatres, schools, and other venues; others have delighted in performing in plays for audiences of all ages. There has been, however, little emphasis placed on documenting or exploring the process of developing scripts written by adult playwrights and performed by and/or for infants, children, and adolescents.

This book shares the insights of over 75 playwrights, artistic directors, dramaturgs, publishers, and other theatre professionals working in the field commonly referred to as Theatre for Young Audiences (TYA). While this book could have been titled *Playwriting for Young Audiences*, we instead use *Playwriting AND Young Audiences* to acknowledge the fact that not all playwrights whose work is eventually seen by young people set out to write specifically *for* young audiences. As our subtitle implies, we embrace a holistic and inclusive approach because it is *not* our goal to give readers definitive answers about what they should and shouldn't do in their practice, but rather to raise issues and explore questions that inform and inspire each reader's individual journey as a voice in the larger community.

This book is for new and established playwrights and theatre professionals of all types, educators working with students of all ages, students learning about the field, and anyone else involved and interested in the intersection of theatre, playwriting, and young people.

For newcomers to TYA this book provides an introduction to the field. It reviews field-specific terminology, offers advice from seasoned professionals, and points to other resources relating to both aesthetic and business aspects of writing in this field.

For seasoned professionals (and those in between), this book offers the opportunity to explore the views of their colleagues working in a variety of positions, on everything from personal philosophies to stances on challenges facing the field.

Experienced playwrights who do not normally write with young people in mind but are curious about TYA may discover ideas for deepening their own work for general audiences. As Karen Zacarías has noted, writing TYA has "pushed me to be more imaginative, more playful, and more sophisticated in my storytelling. [...] TYA naturally lends itself to a magical conceit that translates in original and poetic ways in adult plays" (Zacarías para. 14). We believe other playwrights may find their work similarly enriched by exploring writing in the TYA arena.

How to read this book

Each chapter in this book builds upon and further explores ideas presented in preceding chapters; we therefore highly recommend reading this text sequentially. While each chapter has a clear focus, we frequently refer back to concepts established earlier in the work throughout.

Content and presentation

Interviews

The goal of this book is to provide a wide range of perspectives on issues related to playwriting and young audiences. While we offer our views throughout, the majority of this text is comprised of what we learned by conducting interviews with a wide range of professionals working in the field. We invited artistic directors (including those of all theatres listed in TYA/USA's *Marquee*, a directory of professional TYA companies in the United States), dramaturgs and literary managers active in the field, literary agents, education professionals working with theatre companies, representatives from major publishers who specialize in work for young audiences, and dozens of playwrights at all stages of their careers. While not everyone was able to participate, we include responses from participants representing a broad cross-section of the field.

Nearly all interviews were conducted by email, allowing us to share respondents' views verbatim. While some responses were edited for length, we confirmed with each participant that the revised response reflected her or his original meaning before finalizing this manuscript.

Presentation

The complicated nature of the field resulted in respondents having a wide spectrum of views; all of which we try to include to the extent possible, given space limitations. At times quotes are integrated directly into the narrative text of a paragraph when they are particularly salient or illustrative of a particular point. In most cases, however, answers to questions are listed individually underneath the question that was posed in order to help readers see the variety of views on each question in a clear format. So as not to privilege any particular view, when sharing responses to a particular question we always list responses alphabetically by the respondents' last name. Furthermore, any quote that does not include a parenthetical citation with a page number is from our interviews with the participants. Quotes from published work are always accompanied by a page or paragraph number citation.

Pronouns

Finally, a note about pronouns. Playwrights of all genders work in this field. To avoid the incorrect use of "they" or awkward "he or she/her or his," when referring to playwrights in the singular form we alternate between female and male gender pronouns in the interest of equity. Odd-numbered chapters employ female pronouns; even-numbered chapters use male pronouns.

***

By sharing both research and the personal experiences of our respondents and ourselves, we aim to spark dialogue regarding how quality work performed with, for, and about young people can elevate the TYA field's standing in the larger field of theatre and, more broadly, in society.

We hope that all who read this book – playwrights, other TYA professionals, and all those invested in the field – will join the many respondents who contributed to this book in advancing us all toward that goal.

Chapter 1

Introduction

A mong professionals working in the field of theatre with and for young people, myriad definitions of the term "young audiences" abound. Before we can explore how playwrights might approach work likely to be viewed by young people, we must first understand who young people are and what we mean when we talk about theatre for these individuals. This chapter therefore begins by exploring questions that include:

- Who are young audiences?
- What is Theatre for Young Audiences (TYA)? In what ways is it similar to or different from other types of theatre?
- Is it helpful or problematic (or both) to conceive of TYA as a separate type of theatre – a field distinct from or within the field of theatre more broadly?
- In what ways are the processes of actually writing plays for young audiences similar to or different from writing for other audiences?

Who are young audiences?

The question of who "young audiences" are can be a deceptively complex question; the answer varies based in part on cultural contexts. In the United States, for example, for (most) legal purposes people become "adults" at the age of 18, and as such we might consider anyone 17 or below to be an infant, child, or adolescent. However, people must reach the age of 21 to legally consume "adult beverages," and in many states people gain the "adult" right to drive a motor vehicle as early as age 16. Basing a definition of "young people" on arbitrary and conflicting laws is therefore problematic.

Given the conflicting ages associated with adult activities in the United States, it is not surprising that turning to international organizations for a definition of young people is also challenging. For example, the United Nations (UN) offers different/overlapping definitions of children and youth. The UN Convention on the Rights of the Child, which was ratified by all 197 member nations (except Somalia, South Sudan, and the United States of America), defines a "child" as a "human being below the age of eighteen years unless under the law applicable to the child, majority is attained earlier" (46), suggesting that the maximum age of a "child" is 17, but could be any younger age if an individual nation's laws so dictate. The UN simultaneously defines "the world youth population" as "the age cohort 15–24" (Resolution 50/81, 7). Therefore, as defined by the UN, people in most countries between the ages of 15 and 17 are simultaneously "children" and "youth," and (if these definitions are applied to a US–American context), people between 18 and 24 are both "youth" and "adults."

Clearly, there is no "magical" point at which all human beings transition from one presumed class ("young people") to another ("adults"). While people experience biological changes as they mature, most connotations associated with particular classifications based on age are social constructs: they exist because a critical mass within a society has chosen to adopt them. While these socially accepted definitions and classifications based on age may be artificial constructs, they nevertheless have very tangible effects that create divisions between groups of people, often privileging some while oppressing others. As Lee notes:

> Chronological age is among the axes of human variability that have been linked to the social distribution of dignity and respect. Children can be marked out as a social group, distinguished by the visibility of their low chronological age. Their points of view, opinions and desires have often been ignored because their age has been taken as a sign that they are not worth listening to.
>
> (1)

Similarly, Clark argues that as adults: "We value childhood. But we also dismiss it. We value the image even as we ignore the reality" (1).

Some scholars (e.g., Aries) posit that the notion of children and childhood was an invention of the twentieth century. Before this time, some argue, children were essentially seen as "miniature adults" who worked adult jobs and did not enjoy a space set aside for personal growth and development that many young people do today. That said, references to children as independent entities from adults (even in the context of theatre) can be found as far back as 2500 years ago in the works of Plato, 2000 years ago in the Bible, and throughout the seventeenth and eighteenth centuries as plays specifically for children flourished in some countries, as evidenced by texts such as Stephani de Genlis's 1787 *Theatre of Education*.

While there are many reasons societies have chosen to "mark out" children as a social group of lower status than adults, Kremar follows the work of Burman to posit that in recent years:

> There have been political and economic reasons to assume that children lack knowledge and ability that requires them to have a (female) caretaker for a lengthy time. This results in a freeing of jobs for an adult, male workforce. These social and political forces define childhood, generating assumptions about it: namely that childhood exists, and these assumptions remain embedded in our cultural beliefs about children.
>
> (40)

A number of scholars have analyzed how the arts, including but not limited to theatre, actively contribute to the social construction of childhood. Etheridge Woodson, for example, argues:

> While humans must necessarily experience biological immaturity, childhood is the manner in which a society understands and articulates that physical reality. [...] Like early feminists whose work separated gender from sex and deconstructed understandings of "natural," I am interested in unpacking and exploring the ways in which US culture, and the varied discourses and practices of child drama in the US, shape and understand the "child" and the metaphorical geography of "childhood."
>
> ("Constructing" 132)

At the same time, not all scholars accept the notion that childhood is primarily a social construct. As Kremar, following the work of child psychologists such as Piaget, notes: "one of the most straightforward assumptions that guides work in developmental psychology ... is the assumption that *children are qualitatively different from adults*" (39, emphasis in original).

Recognizing that (A) from a biological perspective, children are different from adults, and that (B) most cultures have constructed notions of childhood that distinguish children from adults, it seems important to determine how TYA professionals define the term "young audiences" and what this classification means to people in the field. Whether or not producers, playwrights, and others in the field consider the people who sit in TYA theatre seats to be "qualitatively different" than those who attend other types of theatre, society's assumption that these audiences are different affects the work TYA artists write, produce, and publish. Below are representative responses we received that illustrate the broad spectrum of ideas held:

How do you personally define the term "young audiences"?

Drew Chappell

"I define 'young audiences' as people from preschool (around age 3) through college age. Yet I'm aware that most of the time, artists and producers define the ideal 'young audience' as between second grade and sixth grade (i.e., old enough to focus on a live performance for an hour and young enough not to wish they were watching something other than material marketed as 'for young audiences.'"

Peter Duffy

"I tend not to think about the term young audiences. I will use the term 'TYA' as a category as I would 'farce' or 'comedy of manners,' but as a targeted group of people, I don't think in that way. I think good theatre is good theatre. If I were to direct The Music Man I wouldn't *call it 'Theatre for Old People'; it's a musical and it has certain demands, appeal, and draw. I don't feel like we do ourselves any favors when we separate the art to become something apart from the broad and vibrant field of theatre."*

Murry Hepner

"I define young audiences as anyone from elementary through middle school ages. I think of High School students and older as being in a different category, maybe 'young adult' audiences. For kids that are not yet in school – I think I'd call them something else: 'Very Young'?"

David Kilpatrick

"For people outside the field, it's easier for me to just say 'children's theater' and avoid a long drawn-out explanation met by blank stares. I don't necessarily get hung up on the negative connotations that others associate with that term. For those who work in the field, I'd say that the term 'young audiences' should mean anything on stage that can play for audiences under the age of 18, whether it's originally intended for young people or not."

Andy Manley

"Quite a few years ago somebody told me you weren't considered an adult, in ancient times, until you were 35. I have an idea it was Plato who said it; I could be wrong though. I like the concept. It makes sense to me. The idea that you are 18 or 21 and are now an adult seems strange. I think it seemed strange to me even when I was 18, but I couldn't have said why. That your theatrical taste will suddenly now be the same as your 70-year-old neighbor seems odd. I have watched shows that have left me cold while the 25-year-olds in the audience have completely loved it. I have seen King Lear *three times in my life but I suspect it will have more impact the older I get. All that said, it probably wouldn't suit funders to believe that 35 was adulthood, it would mean that young companies would take half of the arts budget!"*

Stephani Etheridge Woodson

"I think kids deserve to be treated like humans. Not humans in training."

***

As the quotes above demonstrate, there are discrepancies in terms of how the TYA field is perceived. In the United States, for example, people generally cease to be considered "young audiences" when they reach age 18, while individuals as old as 30 might be considered "young" audience members in some European and Australian contexts.

For the purposes of our book that primarily considers the US–American market, we consider "young audiences" and "young people" to be individuals between the ages of 0 and 17. While recognizing that *any* "dividing line" between "youth" and "adulthood" is arbitrary, needing some way to define the scope of this book, we turn to the constitution of the International Association of Theatre for Children and Young People (ASSITEJ) to ground our definition. The constitution states: "ASSITEJ endorses Article 31 of the 1989 United Nations' Convention of the Rights of the Child that affirms the right of children to leisure time and the enjoyment of arts and cultural activities" (1). Article 31 of the UN Convention referred to in the ASSITEJ Constitution defines a "child" as a person age 17 or under (UN, *Convention* 46).

We also, however, recognize that TYA often functions as an "umbrella term" for numerous more specific types of theatre, such as Theatre for the Very Young (TVY), or Theatre for Teens. As with the general term TYA, these classifications mean different things in different contexts and elude specific, stable definitions; we explore these classifications in greater detail in chapter two. We also posit at this point that TYA is a type of theatre but is *not* a genre, style, or form of theatre. Indeed, TYA can be written and performed in any genre, style, or form, as discussed in the next chapter. For our purposes at present, what sets TYA apart is primarily who is in the audience (which can vary, and again is addressed further in the next chapter). It is also important to note that when we use the term "Youth Theatre" we are referring to material performed by young actors (for any audience).

TYA and theatre for general audiences

Just as there are differences in views concerning who "young audiences" are, when we asked respondents if they felt TYA was (or should be) different than work for general audiences, their views were diverse. Most of the playwrights, artistic directors, publishers, and other theatre professionals we interviewed indicated that, with some exceptions, there are significant differences between TYA and other types of contemporary theatre. At the same time, many of these individuals suggested that TYA *should not* or *ought not* be as removed from theatre for general audiences. In many cases, respondents implicitly or explicitly opined that TYA should not be regarded as a separate type of theatre because of the way theatre associated with young people has been marginalized (as it has been for centuries; texts documenting the history of the field discuss this in detail [e.g., Bedard 2005, van de Water 2012]). We believe, however, that recognizing that TYA has unique properties and has cultivated a field of practitioners who often work primarily or exclusively in TYA neither implies that it is a "lesser" type of theatre than any other, nor that it should be regarded as such.

There is no doubt that theatre with and for young people is currently marginalized by the greater theatre community, as we and our respondents explore in detail below. It is also undeniable, we believe, that the material circumstances of the TYA field are substantively different from those of many other types of theatre. Just as Applied Theatre and Theatre for Social Change share attributes of traditional theatre for general audiences but are clearly different in other respects, so is the case for TYA, and we do not believe that this is a bad thing. What we do believe must change is the way the field is perceived by others in the theatre community and society at large. We write this book in the hope of helping to be a part of that change, which is already under way. The twenty-first century has seen a TYA company win a Regional Tony Award, an issue of *American Theatre* dedicated to the field that largely praised its work, and the production and publication of countless high-quality scripts for young people that have received positive reviews from newspapers around the country. Despite these advances, there is much to be done. We hope that readers of this book will join us and the many professionals who participated in this project in an effort to advance the profile of the field, a goal we know can be achieved.

Differences between TYA and theatre for general audiences

TYA faces gatekeepers not present in other types of theatre; young people are "captive audiences"
While in theatre for general audiences, adults purchase tickets when they have decided that they want to attend a particular performance, this is not the case in TYA. It is individuals, rather (generally educators and parents) who typically decide what theatre productions young people will attend. These adults thereby serve as "gatekeepers," metaphorically standing guard at the theatre's entrance to determine who is permitted to see any given production. As Zacarías notes, "in TYA, the kids are usually present in the audience because someone has brought them, and I feel a deep responsibility to honor their time and their limitations of choice by creating a play that is hopefully relevant to their lives" (para. 13).

Some artists such as Moses Goldberg, while noting that "choice as an element in attending the arts is missing [for school audiences], so some aspects of the school time performance are less than ideal" (*Essays* 172), also accept that gatekeepers "have the right and duty to make judgments about their children's lives [and that he is there] to assist them in reaching those goals" (*Essays* 164–165). Others, like Kim Peter Kovac, argue that TYA companies' assumptions about gatekeepers lead them to engage in a priori censorship. He notes that companies "protect [their] audiences from words, situations, or subjects that [they] have somehow decided are not appropriate or too complex for a particular group. Or, [they] anticipate in advance what the gatekeepers (parents and teachers) will deem inappropriate, and [they] 'protect' based on that" (as quoted in Omasta, "Contract" 111).

Gatekeepers often insist that TYA content be educational. For example, the ASSITEJ Constitution includes a number of objectives that are "inherently teacherly in nature," including "inspiring ethical choices," "encouraging opinions," and "deepening intelligence" (Omasta, "Contract" 106). Bedard similarly notes: "many theatre companies must explicitly foreground their work as educational to catch the attention of school gatekeepers" (97). TYA companies, schools, and parents/communicates have developed an unspoken social contract under which TYA companies commit to:

- Teaching about theatre
- Teaching about social issues and diversity (though, "given the turbulent political climate in the United States, TYA companies must both mark and mask their efforts to educate about diversity")
- Teaching academic curricula
- Engaging in the social construction of childhood that frame children in ways generally aligned with Romantic notions of children. (Omasta "Contract" 107–109)

As such, "much TYA today still posits a white, middle-class, heteronormative 'reality,'" and asks "Who counts as a 'community member' and how/why do we privilege some voices over others?" (Omasta, "Contract" 109).

David Kilpatrick acknowledges that while gatekeepers are powerful, he believes it is sometimes possible for theatres to find ways to produce the work they want without allowing gatekeepers to dictate content. For example, he notes that theatres "can prescribe an educational hook to any story after it's written, and only if needed to justify to a producer or publisher that it can work for young audiences."

While plays for general audiences may include child characters, the majority of TYA and Youth Theatre productions feature child or adolescent protagonists
Most TYA professionals agree that a defining characteristic of TYA is the inclusion of a child protagonist. York notes:

When I write a play for children, there is always an age appropriate character at the center of the action; in other words the main character and pivotal characters are kids. Some of my plays for adults have children at the center of the action; I would never focus on an adult in a play for children, not even an adult looking back, as kids exist in the now and want characters to do that as well.

Brooks agrees, noting: "Your protagonist should be close to the age of the audience you are writing for or slightly older."

Buchanan observes that there are some exceptions to this rule, but maintains that the play must "at very least be about things that young people are concerned with or interested in." Church also notes that there may be exceptions, stating: "a general rule I follow is the play must have a youth protagonist. That said, we are doing several plays in our 2014–15 season that don't necessarily follow this tried and true guideline." Church describes two plays from his current season that do not feature child protagonists, along with the rationale for not following the "general rule" he mentions above.

We are opening with *Rosa Parks and the Montgomery Bus Boycott*, which is a unique take on a documentary play, which adds period civil rights songs sung with gospel arrangements. No youth protagonist, though it's interesting to note Martin Luther King is only 24 years old when this play is set, which nearly counts as a youth protagonist. In Kate DiCamillo's *The Miraculous Journey of Edward Tulane*, Edward Tulane is a prim china rabbit, depicted as a puppet who wears fancy adult-like clothes and is shadowed & voiced by an actor/musician with a guitar. This leads me to say putting together a season is unique, and when writing for TYA, I don't think it's always a must to have a youth protagonist, but there would need to be a unique reason why there isn't one.

TYA playwrights often have their work produced in different venues and published by different publishers, and are often members of organizations that focus solely on TYA
Many theatres across the nation are dedicated exclusively to TYA. While some theatres produce work for general audiences and young people, they often offer only one show for young audiences, and it is generally isolated from the other shows (e.g., not included as an official part of the season, or not included in the season ticket holder package except as an optional add-on, and it is marketed to different audiences). In some cases these shows are not even open to general audiences but only to school audiences, and the source of funding may differ.

Niche publishers specializing in TYA and Youth Theatre markets publish the majority of TYA scripts. Though other major publishing houses may sometimes consider plays for youth, these plays are usually categorized and marketed separately from other plays. Many publishers explicitly state that they do not accept submissions of such work. This ban on TYA submissions also applies to many new play development opportunities, fellowships, grants, and awards.

While TYA playwrights may join professional organizations for general-audience playwrights, they also often join organizations that hold conferences, publish journals, and offer awards and other opportunities specifically related to TYA.

Many TYA professionals train in different academic programs than those preparing to work in theatre for general audiences
A growing number of academic programs around the United States offer training specifically in theatre with and for young people. Especially at the graduate level, many emerging professionals planning to work in TYA and related fields pursue degrees such as an M.F.A. in Theatre for Youth or Ph.D. in Educational Theatre as opposed to more general graduate degrees in theatre (e.g., an M.F.A. in acting or directing). Countless other colleges and universities offer classes, certificates, and undergraduate degrees in TYA, playwriting with and for young people, theatre education, and related fields.

While graduate students in these programs likely take some coursework that is similar or identical to that of their colleagues in acting, directing, or theatre history, the fact that their programs are specialized means that much of their training is qualitatively different from that of their peers. These programs are often taught by faculty who have worked extensively (perhaps exclusively) in the specialization. These students, furthermore, often take courses that help them better understand and prepare to work with young people (both directly within a theatrical context and at times through classes in psychology and/or education), and generally complete thesis/dissertation projects that are specifically geared toward theatre with/for youth. These differences in training mean that these emerging professionals will necessarily have different perspectives of what theatre (in general and with/for youth) has been, is, and could be, than those who did not receive this training but instead specialized in other areas. Ultimately, this means that many people working in TYA received different types of preparation than general theatre professionals and therefore share a common vision of best practices that may differ from their peers in general theatre.

Artists working in TYA are often paid less than their counterparts doing similar work in theatre for general audiences
Unfortunately, while working as a TYA artist is no less challenging than working in general theatre (many argue it is more challenging), financial compensation for TYA work in the field is often less than that in general theatre. While a number of factors contribute to these discrepancies, some major contributors to the problems are the same professional organizations that theoretically advocate for the field. Actor's Equity (AEA), for example, promotes inequity in pay for actors through its use of a specific contract for TYA performances.

Specifically, an actor working under an AEA contract for a League of Resident Theatres (LORT) Theatre (non-rep, outside of NYC) in the month of January 2015 would receive a minimum weekly salary between $935 (LORT A) and $600 (LORT D). However, an actor working under the AEA TYA contract during this same month would earn a minimum salary ranging from only $461 (Tier I Companies) to $452 (Tier II Companies). This means that an actor earning the *highest* minimum salary under a TYA contract would make only 77% of the salary of an actor earning the *lowest* weekly minimum for a non-TYA production under a LORT D contract. The discrepancies only grow from there – for example, an actor making the highest weekly minimum under a TYA contract would make almost 50% less than an actor earning the lowest minimum salary at a LORT A theatre.

Some might contend that it is unfair to compare the TYA agreement to LORT theatre agreements; however, TYA actors are paid less than their counterparts under a variety of AEA contracts that allow producers to pay performers less-than-LORT salaries. For example, AEA's agreement with Disney World specifies that performers must earn a minimum of $651.20 for "chorus stepping out/principal performers"; thus, the Disney minimum is over 40% greater than the TYA Tier I minimum. Even under the Small Professional Theatre AEA contract, an actor performing in a non-TYA production for at least six shows/38 hours per week is guaranteed a higher minimum weekly salary (ranging from $462 for six shows to $645 for eight) than an actor performing in a Tier I TYA production. It should also be noted that while most AEA agreements limit actors to a maximum of eight performances per week, the TYA contract permits up to 12 performances per week (with no additional compensation provided until the tenth performance in a week). AEA stage managers also receive less compensation (for more performances) than their counterparts in other forms of theatre.

Although a side effect of lower pay rates may mean that more TYA companies are able to employ Equity actors and stage managers (for more performances and at a lower cost than other companies), the fact that the professional organization representing actors has negotiated contracts that signify that TYA performers are (literally) worth less than others is problematic. While some might argue that TYA performances are likely to be shorter than other plays, this is not always true. Indeed, many TYA plays are two-act productions that run over two hours while it is not atypical for Broadway and other professional productions to run no more than 90 minutes. The myth that TYA performers inherently put in fewer hours than their counterparts in other types of plays is not supported by evidence.

These pay discrepancies perpetuate a stigma by implying that TYA is a lesser form of theatre. If actors and other professionals are paid less to work in TYA, this material circumstance may lead them to view such work as less desirable and to believe that TYA productions are, by and large, less important than non-TYA productions.

The issue of pay has also arisen specifically in terms of compensation for playwrights. In 1989, a group of theatres formed the New Generation Play Project (NGPP) for the purposes of attracting playwrights who normally wrote for adults to write works for young people. Jennings notes:

> The discussion concerning the generation of new works led to the realization that to persuade exceptional adult playwrights to consider writing for children, project directors would have to overcome two chief obstacles. One hurdle was that most established adult playwrights had seemingly no real reason to write for young audiences, and the other was that *the project directors would have to find means to offer compensation generous enough to appeal to playwrights of the adult theatre.*
>
> (Eight 2, emphasis added)

The theatres partnering in the project sought to overcome these obstacles, but ultimately, the NGPP was unable to meet its goal of attracting eight professional adult playwrights to write for young people. Only half of the playwrights who ultimately agreed to participate were new to writing for young people (Jennings, *Eight* 6). Although there are a variety of reasons playwrights opted not to participate, compensation may have been a factor.

Some emerging artists coming from outside the TYA field who hope to work in theatre for general audiences may perceive working in TYA as a "training ground" to pass time while waiting to work in what they perceive to be "legitimate" theatre
Matt Buchanan argues that there is a problematic American tendency to:

> regard anything related to children as a sort of farm-team prelude to the adult big leagues. We regard with suspicion anyone who deliberately dedicates him/herself to working with or for children. We assume that the dearest ambition of the high school football coach

is to move "up" to college, and that the college coach in turn longs for the NFL. But it's especially prominent in the arts. The average age of performers in professional TYA is much younger than in any other professional company, because these companies are largely treated as training grounds, and the actors inevitably move "up" after a few years.

It's a pretty standard model that folks who make a success with a work of art for children tend to parlay that success into making art for adults – Webber and Rice's first collaboration was a Sunday School pageant. J. K. Rowling is writing for adults now. I'm not suggesting that all, or even most, people who make such a transition necessarily think of it as moving "up" – but the perception is clearly that the importance and glory of any work is proportional to the age of its audience or constituency.

Goldberg notes that it is difficult for theatre artists (of any sort) to find professional work. Given the American theatre scene today, he notes:

> if [emerging artists] are lucky enough to be hired by a high quality TYA company, and they are sensitive to the impact their work has on receptive minds, they will tend to continue in this field. Others never have the exposure, or – if they do – it is to inferior work, so they develop a negative attitude. I would advocate that artist training programs be more aware that many first jobs can be found in TYA, and that they take leadership in preparing their graduates for this work.

David Wood further notes: "Often those who work in TYA are perceived by their peers and the general public to be at the bottom of a ladder, which they hope to ascend soon, into the impressive world of adult theatre!"

Some professionals are emphatically opposed to artists using TYA as a "training ground." As early as 1949, Horton argued: "children's theatre is not to be used as a means of personal advancement, financial aggrandizement, or mere amusement. The question must be asked: Are you good enough to work in children's theatre? Just liking to is not sufficient" (4). Others note that many or most of the people working in TYA choose to do so because they feel called to the work. Wood notes that these "actors, directors, writers, composers, designers, etc. really want to work in this area. They do not see it as something a beginner does, they see it as the career they want to follow."

Benefits of considering TYA as a different type of theatre

We began the previous section by noting that there are differences between TYA and other types of theatre, and that, while we hope to see this change over time, the field is marginalized. Despite the fact that TYA faces this marginalization on a regular basis, respondents also spoke to the positive aspects of thinking of TYA as a separate type of theatre than that for general audiences. We present some such views below:

Rachel Briley

"When I think about the nomenclature Theatre for Young Audiences, something resonates deeply for me: the audience is identified and articulated in the name of discipline. So often when we think about the roles of theatre artists (director, designers, playwright, actor, dramaturg, audience member) we do not take into account the audience – and their role in the theatre-making process. The role of the audience is to construct meaning. I see absolutely no problem with acknowledging that in how TYA self-identifies. It is, in fact, what we do – we create theatre for younger audiences. And that matters because both the audience and children matter. I find it a privilege to work in a field that is focused on children and young people; I celebrate that not only in the work I do, but in the way I speak about what I do. I work in Theatre for Young Audiences – and am so proud to acknowledge it."

Drew Chappell

"I usually draw a comparison between TYA and children's literature. Many if not most adults know what children's literature is: picture books, chapter books, and even young adult novels often focused on young protagonists. These books, from Dr Seuss to Newbery winning young adult novels The Giver *and* Holes *are frequently widely read by both children and adults and made into successful films. Young adult novels such as the Harry Potter series have been massive hits and have garnered wide readerships. In addition, the proliferation in film of superhero stories, fairy tales, fantasy, and science fiction that can be enjoyed by people across ages has begun to break down the barrier between 'young audiences' and 'adult audiences.' I think TYA should be using these texts as a template for what can be produced successfully and uniquely for the stage, creating experiences for children and adults to enjoy together."*

Celise Kalke

"I think that there are many benefits in terms of logistics of viewing TYA as a defined form of theatre. If a work is for a general audience, it can easily drift toward the 90-minute running time mark. This is a more spun out form of storytelling than the TYA 60–70 minutes, and strains some young attention spans. What is beautiful about this one hour form is the guarantee to parents that their child's ability to sit still will be attended to. At the Alliance, our TYA shows use the Atlanta talent pool interchangeably with our adult shows, often allowing multidisciplinary artists greater range. But the production values and acting quality are consistent with any other Alliance production, keeping in mind that the aesthetic demands of children are as immediate and worth valuing as any other patron."

The marginalization of TYA

Above we examined some of the differences between TYA and general theatres. In doing so, issues of marginalization began to present themselves (most notably, perhaps, issues related to financial compensation for TYA artists). In this section, we review further ways in which marginalization is manifested in this arena and discuss specific factors that contribute to this issue. It is not our intent to discourage playwrights or artists from working in the field, but rather to present readers with a realistic view of some challenges they may face and to inspire dialogue about ways to address and combat some of the misperceptions and other factors that have led to this reality. It is our hope that in exploring these issues, passionate TYA artists and practitioners will identify opportunities and find motivation to break down existing barriers.

To begin, even theatre leaders outside the TYA field recognize the way TYA can be viewed. Former Theatre Communications Group (TCG) Executive Director Ben Cameron notes: "Unfortunately, those who have given their lives to TYA and to education programming are often dismissed by others in the field [of theatre generally] – viewed with condescension or tolerance, seen as doing work that is a sop to public funding but somehow distinct from 'real' work" (as quoted in Bedard 97).

Debbie Devine points to "the lack of respect the sector has, which is made evident in that the largest US professional theatre membership organization (TCG) doesn't even include TYA in their annual conference." Indeed, most national organizations related to theatre practice and/or scholarship largely ignore TYA as demonstrated through a relative lack of permanent focus groups, conference sessions, and publications related to the field. As of March 2015, no LORT theatres defined themselves as being primarily dedicated to theatre for young audiences, adolescents, or family audiences, though most had offerings during their season or through an education department for one or more of those audience groupings.

In order to combat further marginalization of their work, practitioners in the field must understand the forces at play contributing to it. Earlier in this chapter we discussed the notion that any work associated with children is often seen by society as "less than" – as Lee wrote: children's age "has been taken as a sign that they are not worth listening to" (1). It logically follows that some in society will have doubts about adults who *do* listen to children and take them seriously.

Media coverage

Another contributor to the field's marginalization is the relative lack of coverage afforded to TYA productions by the media, especially when compared to general-audience theatre productions in the same communities. While not the case in every locale, as Mary Rose Lloyd points to Lyn Gardner who notes,

There are companies creating quality works for young audiences that are not getting the attention and respect they deserve. This lack of coverage matters because it is always the case that what is reviewed in our culture quickly becomes what is valued in our culture. An absence of reviews about theatre that is made for and with children, and a reluctance by arts desks and editors to take children's theatre seriously not only suggests that we do not value that particular area of theatre, but that we do not value children and their experience of the world. It shouldn't be that way.

This dearth of coverage is hardly new. Writing in 1974, Lifton argued: "Somewhere along the line [TYA] has given up, stopped protesting its segregated status, settled for second best. The result is that children's theatre is looked on with disdain by critics who do not review it" (12). Regardless of whether or not practitioners at large had "given up" (the 1970s actually saw the development of several new initiatives in TYA), the lack of media coverage Lifton mentions is still prevalent.

The challenges TYA companies face getting media coverage may also stem from misconceptions as to exactly what constitutes this type of theatre. Noting that theatre journalists are candidly confused as to what "TYA" actually means, Cooney, Green, and Kramer explain:

> a surprising number or journalists assume TYA means performances by children alone, a characterization that sets off alarms. [...] Of course, the explanation that TYA can include performances by children acting alone or alongside adults, or adults cast as children, or solo actors, or puppets, does little to resolve the confusion.
>
> (13)

To be fair, troubles with media coverage are contextually dependent. Even *The New York Times*, for example, does sometimes review TYA productions in NYC; in other locations where other theatres are located, however, newspapers do not review TYA at all.

Funding

TYA may also be marginalized by a lack of funding. As mentioned earlier, many major playwriting awards and other opportunities are not open to playwrights writing for young people. Furthermore, David Wood notes:

> Theatre directors, critics, drama schools, the general public and the theatrical profession in general perceive theatre for children as something less important that adult theatre. Part of this is to do with money. Children's theatre rightly does not charge as much for tickets as adult theatre. Very often actors are paid less when they work in a children's play. Children's theatre cannot generate enough box office income to balance the books. It often needs sponsorship or subsidy.

In the United States, where the budget of the National Endowment for the Arts must defend its budget annually against repeated threats of (or actual) cuts, TYA companies have few government subsidies to which they may turn. As described in detail above, actors, stage managers, and even playwrights frequently are paid less than their colleagues working in theatre for general audiences.

Internal prioritization in general-audience theatres

As indicated above, there are a number of non-TYA-specific theatres throughout the country that sometimes produce TYA shows. Murry Hepner points out, however, that:

> Unfortunately, there are still some companies who perpetuate the marginalization of the field by *not* giving their children's programming the same priority as their other work. TYA incorporates all the thought, planning, artistry and creativity of all theatre (or it should). If it doesn't, then people will continue to think of it as "less than" mainstream theatre.

Regardless of the type of company producing the work, Celise Kalke states: "I think a drawback happens when acting or production values suffer because of the production budgets TYA shows receive." Of course, this corresponds to the trouble with funding in general. Ultimately, a number of factors entangle TYA in a complex web that perpetuates the marginalization of the field, its practitioners, and its products.

Self-marginalization

Peter Duffy notes that TYA practitioners themselves contribute to the field's marginalization, arguing:

> It is problematic to segregate TYA from other types of theatre. I think when we make TYA too precious and too dear to our own individual identity as theatre artists, we diminish the vibrancy of the broad art form of theatre. If we make our field something that only the initiated understand, then we create silos of meaning and experience. I want to work in the other direction to demonstrate how expansive the existing language of the theatre is so that when a specific term is used, it by its very nature includes TYA.

There is also a contention that TYA is not, in fact, as marginalized as it may seem, but appears to be simply because people do not yet understand what it is. Michael J. Bobbitt states:

> I believe that TYA is already mainstream, but the field doesn't necessarily embrace all of its parts. TYA, including all of its sub-forms (e.g., family theatre, TVY, etc.), is the largest growing, if not the largest most influential field of theatre existing. Broadway is overrun by theater adapted from works originally created for children. In any given year, there are 5–8 Broadway TYA shows. This is having a major effect on regional theatres. I'd be surprised to find any LORT theatre in this country not producing a TYA show each season.

If this is the case, then those working in TYA must collectively address perceptions by working through the web of ways in which the field *is* marginalized, until others in the broader theatre community and eventually society at large understand the work in the field and its potential (and actual) accomplishments.

TYA as a unique field

We understand both sides of the debate regarding the benefits and dangers of treating TYA as a distinct type of theatre. We believe, however, that the material circumstances of the field require that we investigate it separately from the field of theatre for general audiences, while acknowledging that it is, in fact, part of that broader art form. Though some practitioners and scholars might wish that TYA were regarded no differently from theatre for general audiences, in the particular context of the United States in the twenty-first century, forces with greater social and political capital actually define the field for us. These forces include publishing companies (both in theatre and literature), producing and educational entities, funding agencies, labor unions, and professional organizations within and beyond the theatre world. In turn, other forces work upon each of these entities. But perhaps the most powerful entity, in which nearly all of us are complicit to varying degrees, is our society. As in many societies, the powerful (in this case, adults), generally conceive of people under a certain age as a separate class of individuals with different rights, needs, and vulnerabilities, as discussed by Lee and others above.

Publishing companies segregate "children's literature" and "young adult literature" from the broader class of publications considered "literature." In reality, though, adults frequently read these books (consider the popularity among adults of series such as *The Hunger Games*, for example). When adults read these books, however, they are not re-classified as adult literature. *The Hunger Games*, after all, is published by Scholastic, which defines itself on the main page of its website as "the largest *children's book* publisher" and notes that it "promotes literacy with books for *kids* of all ages and reading levels" (emphasis added). Publishers in the playwriting field draw these same distinctions.

Although we acknowledge the contested and problematic nature of age-based classifications, as pragmatists interested in exploring playwriting and young audiences, we must somehow define the scope of our investigation into "young audiences." Additionally, in exploring the relationships between theatre and young people, we rely on commonly accepted understandings (artificial or not) from our own cultural context (the United States in the early twenty-first century) to bound our investigation. Given these overwhelming societal influences that allow adults to construct notions of children as being separate from and other than the adult population, it would be impossible to discuss playwriting for young people without noting the inherently separate sphere in which TYA and Youth Theatre operate. Again, *different* does not mean "worse," and as Michelle Wright notes: "the 'children's theater' stigma is finally wearing thin, and people are seeing our work for the artistry that it is." Indeed, the quality of TYA plays and productions should rival that of any other theatre productions, yet we must recognize that the field is unique.

Differences in writing for young and general audiences

Having established that we view TYA as a unique type of theatre, we next turn to the question of if and how writing with young audiences in mind might differ from writing for general audiences. As early as 1949, practitioners realized even if there were differences, one thing to be avoided was "talking down" to children, who are capable of understanding much more than they are given credit for by some adults. Mitchell writes:

> Talking and writing "down to the supposed child capacity" may cause failure. They may or may not agree with the author of *Androcles and the Lion* that that play is for children; yet directors have proved [...] that children are often able to appreciate situations "of adult depth or deeper."
>
> (19)

Decades later Aurand Harris agreed: "Often I am told, 'How wonderful that you don't write down to children.' This never occurs to me, as I don't know how to 'write down' to a child. I never try to be 'childlike'. I write to please myself as an adult" (as quoted in Jennings, *Six* 21). Jennings goes on to explain, "Harris emphasizes the fact that he likes what children like in the theatre, that is, a good story, interesting characters, excitement, suspense, fantasy, beauty, and fun. Correspondingly, he is opposed to patronizing attitudes toward children" (*Six* 21).

Just as Harris stated that "he likes what children like in the theatre," Goldberg in 1974 noted: "To the playwright then there is no difference in writing for children and writing for adults – at least for the first draft of the script. In both cases he is initially writing for himself" (*Children's* 122–123). As to whether children and adults appreciate the same dramatic material, in 1974 Lifton wrote:

> Let us consider the unsettling aversion that, while there may be a narrow band of experience which only children can appreciate, and another narrow band which only adults can appreciate, there is a vast everyman's land in between where children and adults can appreciate together, though perhaps on different levels. After all, the great children's classics are those which both adults and children enjoy.
>
> (25)

The idea that many stories are understood and appreciated by people of all ages is affirmed by our earlier discussion of literature and film theoretically for young audiences that is actually enjoyed by adults.

More recently, Zacarías noted that perhaps one difference between TYA and theatre for general audiences is that, rather than TYA not needing to meet the same standards as general-audience productions, work for young people may in fact need to be *better* than other types of theatre. She notes: "Plays for children must have all the qualities of a good adult play and then ... something more" (para. 9). She goes on to offer three reasons; the first is: "Children are very constructive critics. [...] If something does not ring true, a young audience protests *instantly*. [...] Kids will not politely allow themselves to be bored. Ever" (Zacarías para. 10). She then notes:

> TYA artists maintain very high, demanding standards even when under tremendous pressure to deliver high quality accessible art from parents, teachers, boards, or their broader organizations. [...] The commitment to integrity raises the artistic stakes and the passion raises the personal stakes – and stress.
>
> (Zacarías para. 12)

Finally, she argues that "the stakes in TYA are much higher, not in terms of royalties or reviews, but in the impact on the audience. A great TYA play can change a young person's life by offering an inspiration, insight, or perspective he or she never had before" (Zacarías para. 13). With these varying thoughts in mind, we asked respondents, including those who do write for both young people and general audiences:

Does the process of writing plays for young people differ in any way from writing plays for adults?

Michael J. Bobbitt

"Theatre is theatre, period. Good theatre is good theatre and bad theatre is bad theatre. One style of theatre is not *better or more important than another style of theatre. Theatre has a multitude of styles that require additional techniques, skills and ways of thinking. No director, actor, designer, producer would approach a Chekov production like they would a musical. Where interpretations of productions sometimes go wrong can often be linked to the artist's non-commitment to the inherent style of the show or the artists on the production not having the skills needed to carry off the style of the production. And if we are being honest, no one approaches TYA the way they approach other types of theatre. In fact, they do consider additional techniques, skills, and ways of thinking."*

Mark Lutwak

"All good theatre should treat its audience as if it were intelligent and as if the theatre experience was a conversation between equals. At its best, TYA shines in how truly aware it is of its audiences: their needs, their concerns, and their intelligence. As such, it can be the

most artistically challenging work out there, in form and content. Most 'adult' playwrights could learn from this attention to the audience's half of the conversation equation. Sadly, most plays for youth actually produced do not demonstrate that level of art or craft. Those with the ability are not listening; those who care for their audiences do not necessarily demonstrate the professional expertise."

Judy Matetzschk-Campbell

"I do not believe that writing for plays for young people is really any different from writing plays for adults, except I think the plays have to be better. By that I mean that a writer working for our audience has to really understand how to activate dialogue. Every word needs to really mean something to the story in a play for young audiences. I think that the only real difference is that, in my opinion, a play written for a young audience needs to leave the audience with a sense of hope for today and for tomorrow. I think a writer working for an adult audience can leave a group of adults in total despair if that is what they want to do and if that is the story they want to tell. But I think plays for child audiences have a responsibility to provide honest hope that tells us as an audience that the young protagonist can overcome the obstacles that face them."

Jonathan Price

"When I write for adults, I write for myself as an audience member, assuming there are probably other adults in the world with my taste. When I write for young people, I keep one eye to my usual process, because I know there will be adults in the audience, but feedback from youth audiences becomes as important as my own opinion. Although I can write something that might have appealed to me as a youth, it doesn't mean it will appeal to the current generation."

Psalmayene 24

"In my experience, writing plays for young people differs, and does not differ, from writing plays for adults. It differs because, obviously, there are certain language restrictions that are in place when you write for young people. Profanity, of course, is out of the question. Long, wordy soliloquies are generally kept at arm's length. And language that is over the head of your audience is wisely avoided. This is not to say that complex ideas cannot be addressed in plays for young people, because they can, and, in an increasingly complicated world, they should be. But they must be expressed in a cognitively digestible way that connects with the audience. I don't dumb down material for young people, but strive to make the complex simple. It's a fun challenge.

I've also found that writing plays for young audiences demands that playwrights organically include a robust amount of theatricality in order to hook, and keep, the audience's attention for the entirety of a production. In writing plays for adults, playwrights can *sometimes afford to be cheap on theatricality without running the risk of losing the attention of the audience. Playwrights who skimp on theatricality for young audiences do so at their own (and their play's) peril.*

In terms of the similarities, for me, respect for the craft of playwriting is equal for both writing plays for young people and writing plays for adults. One still has to deal with action, exposition, conflict, character, and all the other components of playwriting. One still has to attempt to find and illuminate the soul of the play, regardless of the audience. One still must grapple with their demons during the writing process. Ultimately, a poorly written play, whether it's for youth or adults, is just a bad play. Likewise, a well-written play, no matter the audience, will stand up as a beautiful piece of art."

Jonathan Rand

"More often than not, even the most rudimentary attributes of an adult play are the polar opposite of those for young people. In recent years, plays for adults tend to skew toward a tiny cast (given how payroll increases with cast size), envelope-pushing R-rated material, and a running time of around two hours. At the other end of the spectrum, young performers (at a middle school, for instance) usually require a large cast to involve the most students, appropriate content for that age group, and a far shorter running time. The two types of plays rarely intersect."

Greg Romero

"As someone who wrote for adults for almost 15 years before writing a TYA work, I was surprised the process wasn't very much different. While writing my first young audiences play I battled my initial fears by making notes to myself about things I felt I should be especially aware of: I wanted to keep the play active, to only have characters speak words if they absolutely needed to (let the action tell the story), to keep the stakes really high, to create impossible, challenging, empathic journeys, to offer really imaginative worlds, to always be truthful, and to offer as many ways as possible for audience to participate with the event.

After thinking all this through, it became really clear to me – these are things I want and hope for all plays, not just TYA. The only significant difference I've found in writing for adults versus young people is in understanding and expressing the appropriate content within this approach, particularly when exploring the necessary dark sides of a story or character. Certainly there are things that are not appropriate or healthy for young audiences to experience, but keeping those things out of the writing has been an easy adjustment for me, especially knowing I can always go back later and edit out material that isn't good for the play or the people experiencing it."

Suzan Zeder

"I have always said that I do not write for young audiences, I write about young people. I think it is dangerous and potentially condescending and prescriptive for a playwright to

write for any audience. It might sound absurd to hear a playwright say he or she is writing for white, middle-aged, upper income women, yet that is who makes up a big majority of audiences for commercial theatre, particularly Broadway."

***

In sum, respondents had a wide range of views, with some indicating that writing with young people in mind was fairly similar to writing for any other audience, some indicating the processes were polar opposites, and some arguing that the concept of writing *for* an audience is inherently problematic. A consistent theme, however, was that writing TYA is just as difficult (if not more so) and demands just as high a level of craftspersonship as writing any other piece of dramatic literature.

Conclusion

In this chapter we reviewed the contested terrain of what constitutes "young audiences" and the field of TYA. We discussed both the benefits of understanding TYA as a distinct type of theatre and the numerous factors contributing to the marginalization of the field. Finally, respondents debated if and how writing plays with young audiences in mind differs from composing work for general audiences. The comprehensive conclusion reached by all invested parties throughout the chapter is the emphasis on the idea that the *quality* of work in the field must always be equal to (or even greater than) that in any other type of theatre.

As we discussed earlier, TYA is an umbrella term that covers a wide range of approaches to theatre with and for young people. In the next chapter we address these many classifications within TYA in greater detail, exploring the opportunities and limitations of each.

Chapter 2

Genre, Style, and Form

In the last chapter we discussed a number of issues related to theatre, playwriting, and young people. While our respondents expressed a variety of perspectives regarding what we refer to as TYA, for the purposes of this book, we consider TYA a *type* of theatre. It is not a genre, style, or form, but indeed can take on any genre, style, or form. Each of these terms is slippery, and the definitions of each vary depending on which textbook or theatre expert one consults. In order to provide a point of reference for our discussion in this chapter, we offer working definitions below.

For our purposes, *genre* describes a play's nature and content; basic genres include comedy, tragedy, drama, and tragicomedy. *Style* refers to the mode of expression employed, including styles such as realism, naturalism, expressionism, surrealism, theatricalism, and magical realism. *Form* refers to defining mechanisms built into the play, such as song (musical theatre and opera), puppetry, mime, mask, or audience participation. A play of any genre can be presented in any style and form (or even multiple forms), for example: a musical tragicomedy in the style of theatricalism, with puppets.

TYA, like any other type of theatre, can be written in any of these genres and presented in all styles and forms. For example, regarding genre: Laurie Brook's *The Wrestling Season* could be considered a drama, Len Jenkin's *Ramona Quimby* a comedy, and Melissa Cooper's *Antigone Now* a tragedy. In terms of style: Barry Kornhauser's *This is Not a Pipe Dream* could be considered expressionism, Pamela Sterling's *The Secret Garden* realism, and Stephen Dietz's *Still Life with Iris* magic realism. Plays can also be produced in many forms (e.g., *Beauty and the Beast* has been developed as a musical [for Disney by Menkin, Ashman, Rice, and Woolverton], as a puppet theatre production [by Steven's Puppets], and as a British pantomime [by Lorraine Mason]). Again, the primary point is that TYA itself is *not* a genre, style, or form.

There are a number of important types of theatre beyond those above that we do not address in-depth because they are outside the scope of our book due to the specificity of their modes of creation and/or presentation. For example, an increasing number of pieces (both in TYA and the broader theatre world) are devised, meaning they "originate with the group while making the performance, rather than starting from a play text that someone else has written to be interpreted" (Oddey 1). Other plays are ethnographic in nature, so while they may be written by a small team of playwrights they actually involve large numbers of participants (e.g., interviewees, focus group participants, etc.). Sarah Myers notes: "TYA companies are employing a wide variety of ethnographic techniques. They use personal storytelling and interviews, participation in community rituals, and even interactive dramaturgy sessions to create original performances" (6). Playwrights interested in this type of dramatic writing may wish to consult Johnny Saldaña's *Ethnotheatre* and *Ethnodrama*. There are also individual approaches that blend aspects of these. Topics discussed throughout this book can be easily applied to devised plays, those employing ethnographic approaches, etc.

Another type of performance we do not explore at length due to its venue and blended mission is museum theatre, which involves "the use of theatre and theatrical techniques as a means of mediating knowledge and understanding in the context of museum education" (Hughes, Jackson, and Kidd 680). Such work generally serves Horace's ancient maxim: to instruct and delight (with perhaps greater emphasis on instruction in many cases). These plays are (naturally) performed in museums, usually before multigenerational audiences, though some museums may commission work specifically for school-day crowds of young people.

Classifications within TYA and Youth Theatre

The term "Theatre for Young Audiences" was developed to replace the outmoded term "children's theatre," which, while popular for perhaps a century, now makes many practitioners in the field cringe. The term is too generic to be meaningful, as it simultaneously connotes theatre for children, by children, both, or something else entirely based on one's past experiences. Furthermore, "children's theatre" has come to signify "bad work" to many people, conjuring up images of men dressed as Captain America encouraging recycling or clowns performing in elementary school gymnasiums. Artists in the field recognized this as a problem several decades ago:

> To clarify the label for both the profession and the general public, the national Children's Theatre Association of America (CTAA) officially adopted an expanded definition of terms. The vague description of "children's theatre" was replaced with "Theatre for Young Audiences," which encompasses both "Theatre for Children" … and "Theatre for the Young."
>
> (Jennings, *Plays* 3)

Of course, the term, while clarifying that it refers to theatre *for* young audiences (as opposed to theatre *written by* or *performed by* young people, remains unclear with regard to exactly who is included in that category of "young" audiences. Creating such definitions can be difficult because, as Barry Kornhauser notes:

> Whereas there are undoubtedly common cultural and developmental benchmarks shared by any two groups of say 3rd to 5th graders, their differences will far outweigh their similarities. For that matter, this is certainly also true of the two 4th graders sitting next to each other in the theater. Each will surely get something unique and special, all his or her own, from your play.

While inter- and intra-age group differences are undeniable, as discussed above there are nevertheless classifications that have emerged in the field based on practice, although they are constantly shifting and not every producer, publisher, or writer adheres to them.

Age-of-audience classification

It is clear that the spectrum of audiences included within TYA specified in our last chapter (0–17) is broad, and that material that appeals to infants may not attract teenage audiences. While there are no definitive, universally agreed upon categories within the field, several methods of classifying work have emerged from working practice in the field, discussions amongst colleagues at professional conferences and symposia, and guidelines developed by producers and publishers. We present a brief overview of these below, again cautioning that they should be viewed as fairly malleable.

One common way to classify plays for young audiences is by the age of the intended audiences (though of course, plays may not always actually appeal most to their "intended" audience). For example, some commonly accepted divisions include:

- Theatre for the Very Young (TVY), also known as theatre for early years, and theatre for very young audiences. Approximately ages 0–5.
  Some further divide this into:
  - Theatre for infants, or baby theatre, approximately ages 0–2
  - Theatre for Pre-K audiences, approximately ages 3–5
- Theatre for Young Audiences (TYA). Approximately ages 5–17.
  Some further divide this into:
  - Theatre for early elementary audiences, approximately ages 5–7
  - Theatre for upper elementary audiences, approximately ages 8–10
  - Theatre for junior high/"tweens," approximately ages 11–13
  - Theatre for teens, approximately ages 13–18 (some theatres market their work for teens separately, under the assumption that teenagers would not want to see work branded as TYA).
- Family Theatre. Strives to appeal all ages: children, adolescents, and adults alike. "This is the same "family market" companies such as Disney target through their animated films."

Interestingly, many of the classifications above are (relatively) new to the field. Writing in 1981, Jennings noted that both very young audiences and older audiences had been neglected: "Most of the dramatic literature has been aimed at [...] students in the late elementary grades [...] with the assumption that many younger and older students would also be interested in the material. [...] Major playwrights have avoided writing for both very young children and children of the junior high school ages" (Jennings, *Plays* 5).

Today, many playwrights are excited to write for teens and the very young. Melissa Cooper comments that she has "had marvelous experiences writing plays specifically for teen audiences. I like to write from the point of view of a teenager in a difficult situation, sometimes, literally, life-and-death, as with *Antigone* or the young combat soldier in *Red Badge Variations.*" Regarding work for the very young, Emily Freeman states: "I think TVY is starting to shift our perceptions and expectations. It is presenting exciting challenges and dialogue around how we write facilitation, interactivity, and participatory moments in scripts. I find this new form of playwriting exciting and challenging!"

The fact that TVY has flourished in the United States over the past decade, and that theatre for middle-school students and teens continues to grow speaks to the constantly evolving nature of the field and the fact that any definitions or classifications offered must necessarily be open to frequent revision. Of course, while some things change others remain the same; as Michelle Wright notes: "the 'bread and butter' age group for children's theatres, the 5–12 year olds, continues like a juggernaut with so many great works coming out."

Despite the various categories delineated above, some playwrights historically and today advocate not trying to write for any particular age, as a well-written play will gravitate toward the appropriate audience. For example:

> If the material is dramatic, Aurand Harris believes that a play "will find its own age level." He does not attempt to write for a specific age or grade. "It is true that in children's theatre there are age differences which must be considered, but many a good children's plays appeal to a wide age range. The nine-year-old and the young teen-ager often like the same script, but for different reasons. In a successful play, children of many ages as well as adults can find something that is satisfying for each of them."
>
> (Jennings, *Six* 21)

It is worth noting that even if a playwright does attempt to write for audiences of a particular age (or a certain venue, or even performers of a certain age), they may find that potential producers of their work feel it is appropriate for an entirely different audience, venue, etc. In such cases, playwrights who wish to see their work brought to the stage may discuss their concerns with the producer, but ultimately will likely need to yield to the views of the theatre, which is investing financially in mounting the production.

Performer-based classification

This book covers writing two types of plays: those that will primarily be seen by young audiences (TYA) and those meant to be *performed by* young people (Youth Theatre). Though there are caveats (described below), in general this book refers to TYA as plays that are written to be performed by professional actors (usually adults, sometimes adults and professionally trained young people) who produce work for audiences primarily composed of children, adolescents, or families (usually under the auspices of a professional theatre company, either in its own performance space or as part of a touring production).

Youth Theatre plays, on the other hand, are explicitly designed to be performed by young people, usually in either community or educational settings (e.g., schools, religious organizations, education programs within professional theatres, etc.). We refer to a play/performance as Youth Theatre *only* when the young actors are amateurs. Broadway productions such as *Annie, Billy Elliot, Matilda,* and *Newsies*, in which even the youngest performers are generally members of Actors Equity (the professional union of actors and stage managers in the United States), are clearly professional TYA/Family Theatre. In 2013, *The New York Times* reported that nine Broadway shows featured professional child actors (Pogrebin). Professionally trained young performers also appear (usually alongside professional adults) in regional theatres throughout the country; the practice employing paid young performers can be traced to at least the nineteenth century in the United States.

Of course, there are always exceptions to these general principles. For example, many non-professional groups (e.g., community theatres) produce TYA. Such performers may include solely amateur adult actors or a mix of adult and child amateurs, resulting in hybrid of TYA/Youth Theatre in performance (though if the script was not written primarily for young performers, we would generally still identify that script itself as a TYA script). Furthermore, a Youth Theatre group (comprised entirely of young amateur actors) could produce a TYA script (with children playing all adult roles, etc.); in such a situation we might say that a TYA script was being performed in a Youth Theatre venue. In theory, a professional company of actors could create a similar hybrid by casting professional adult actors in a production of a Youth Theatre script, but this would be extremely rare; we are unaware of any precedent for this (nor was it mentioned by any of our respondents).

TYA and Youth Theatre have much in common, but also a number of distinct differences. For the purposes of this book, we use the term TYA whenever we are referring either to TYA exclusively or principles that apply to both TYA and Youth Theatre. When discussing topics where recommendations vary based on the type of theatre, we specifically note which form we are discussing, usually comparing and contrasting TYA and Youth Theatre in that particular context.

***

This chapter reviewed the similarities and differences between TYA and Youth Theatre, and provided a detailed classification system that can be used to understand various ways artists, producers, and publishers sometimes break their audiences into groups. Again, there are no definitive groups, and classifications change frequently, but this guide can help new playwrights understand ways that young audiences are sometimes grouped. In the next chapters we will begin to discuss various issues playwrights should consider when writing TYA; we explore ethical concerns in chapter three and practical concerns in chapter four. Because chapter four builds on the ideas in chapter three, we strongly encourage reading them sequentially.

Chapter 3

Ethical Considerations

All writers – all people – are guided by their personal ideologies – their beliefs about the way the world works, their attitudes, values, and moral systems. Humans' ideologies are reflected in everything we do, including writing; as such, each playwright's "writing voice" is informed by her ideology. Playwrights can strive to be honest with themselves about how their beliefs influence their writing. They may even make deliberate efforts to include multiple perspectives in their work. Ultimately, however, it is important that they ask themselves: "what is this play saying?" and realize that it is *always* saying *something*. They should consider what messages are embedded in their work (including any that they may not have intended), and ask themselves if these are messages they want to be sharing with young people.

We present here four examples of how ideology can play a role in theatre productions. The point in each example is not to argue that a particular ideology is "right" or "wrong" but simply to note that it is always present and affects plays and (ultimately) audiences.

1. Sondheim and Lapine's *Into the Woods* interweaves a number of fairy tales, exploring what happens as the protagonists set out to fulfill their wishes. Act I ends with nearly everyone quite content, ready to experience their "happy ever after." Act II, then, explores what happens *after* "ever after," including murder, adultery, and all manner of dark acts. When Music Theatre International (MTI) developed a "junior" version of the show for middle-school-aged performers, in addition to adjusting vocal parts, they cut the second act entirely. Surely this was done in part due to time constraints (the show is supposed to run roughly 60 minutes). It also has the effect (intended or not) of completely changing the meaning of the show. From an ideological perspective, it connotes a belief that "young people can't handle" this sort of material (despite the likelihood that they see similar material frequently on television and in other media), or that gatekeepers (parents, schools) might feel uncomfortable having their children participate in a play with such content.

2. Matetzschk-Campbell and Newman, introducing the plays of Sandy Asher, note: "Each of her plays holds the promise of hope, an element Asher finds essential in TYA. Asher states, 'Childhood and adolescence are not just difficult times; they are times of hope […]. No one can tell children that life is not worth living'" (xii). Though quite different from the example above, the notion that plays must be hopeful and should instill in youth the idea that life is worth living is also ideological. It is a personal belief (albeit one likely shared by many) that guides Asher's work.

3. John Cariani's play *Almost, Maine* has been among the most frequently produced plays in high schools for several years running. The play is comprised of a series of short scenes of couples in love. One of these scenes depicts two male characters who, while never referencing anything sexual, discover they are in love. Many schools that produce this play choose to (illegally) eliminate this scene; in at least one school that we are familiar with, the teacher explicitly stated that she had cut the scene due to the "homosexual content." This is an ideological act. Regardless of one's feelings about gay marriage or any other political topic, one could argue that by cutting this scene from the play a teacher tells her students (some of whom are likely to be LGBTQ youth themselves): "Gay people don't belong in a love story." This is a profound thing for a teacher to say to her students of all sexual orientations.

4. On a completely different note, "Because experiencing a play in the theatre can become a lifelong memory for a child, [Aurand] Harris carefully evaluates the subject matter and inherent ideas. The thought underlying the play must be of enduring positive value that makes it worthy of keeping in mind" (Jennings, *Six* 21). The idea that all plays must be based on an "enduring positive value" is also ideological, and brings with it assumptions about what young people can and cannot handle and what type of work best serves them.

José Casas explains that the ideology of producers can sometimes conflict with that of an individual playwright, noting:

> Every playwright writes to see their stories come to life on the stage. Every playwright wants to be totally unimpeded when it comes to their art, but there is a reality in theatre. If you look at the landscape of TYA there are trends and you see what is being produced. Mainstream TYA theatres are trying to create seasons that allow them to survive and reach out to youth.

Given companies' need to produce work that allows for that survival, Casas poses the question:

> How willing are these theatres to produce work that deals with issues that don't fall into the category of "happy happy" theatre? It's complex and some theatres are more willing to take challenges than others, but I don't think the majority do.

Ultimately, Casas says:

> I believe playwrights have to believe in themselves and their words. I think playwrights should be aware of the realities and difficulties of dealing with the demographics of which they write, but they should also be brave and tell the stories they need to tell. True art is honest art. My opinion is playwrights need to create the art that matters to

them. Hopefully, there will be theatres that believe in what they are trying to say and give them the opportunities. Once a writer falls prey to "what is expected" they are doing themselves and audiences a disservice.

Alternatively, Dorothy Webb notes that sometimes being aware of a producer's ideologies can help playwrights decide where to submit their work or perhaps how to shape it. She notes:

If you are a playwright who is submitting your work to a theatre or a contest, knowing any particular "slants" they may have could save you time, money, and maybe even heartache. Knowing that a theatre is known for plays with strong female protagonists, for example, should be an indication that a play with all men would not be welcomed. To the extent that a writer decides to write to the "agenda" then the whole process will be informed by that agenda. Perhaps the most restrictive agenda, however, is the one a playwright carries in his/her own mind.

Ideology is neither inherently "good" nor "bad," but it always *is*. It affects each of the ethical issues explored in this chapter: questions of diversity, representation, and cross-cultural writing; how practitioners might address controversial or taboo topics; and the implications of adults writing child characters.

Diversity and cultural representation

For centuries, western playwrights largely assumed that they were writing for a fairly homogenous audience. While there are several notable exceptions, until the mid-twentieth century, many American TYA playwrights wrote primarily for audiences of presumably white, straight, able-bodied children from (in most cases) families affluent enough to bring them to the theatre (or to send them to schools that would fund such work). While the demographic makeup of the United States has changed drastically over the past century, in some ways its plays have not.

Today few would dispute that the extant canon of TYA literature fails to equitably represent stories of various cultures or include sufficient contributions from playwrights of color. While reflecting a trend in American theatre more broadly, it is still the case that, as Laurie Brooks notes: "We desperately need more playwrights of color to write for TYA. Currently, there is simply not enough diversity in the field."

The question of how to broaden the canon has sparked a number of debates. For example, can anyone write a play about any culture, regardless of whether or not they are a member of it? Or is the ability to write authentically about a culture only accessible to its members? In a 2008 article, Roxanne-Schroeder Arce addresses this issue specifically in the context of Latina/o TYA. She discusses various reactions to Wendy Kessleman's play *Maggie Magalita*, the story of a teenage Latina (Kessleman herself is not Latina). Schroeder-Arce notes that

Kessleman "felt comfortable writing a play about a culture different from the one into which she was born because of her experiences with people of the culture." On the other hand, Lorenzo Garcia, who "has directed [the play] and enjoyed packed houses of Latino audiences" states that although "'Wendy came up with a form and content that is recognized by Latino audiences" he nevertheless "feels that because Kessleman is not Latina, hers is not a Latino play." Schroeder-Arce goes on to note that this boundary is not always so simple, citing authors such as José Cruz González who points out that "one's race, ethnicity and culture are not always visible," and Latina playwright Karen Zacarías who "says she is proud of the plays she has written about the Latino culture, [she] feels they can't just be termed 'Latino' plays" (Schroeder-Arce, "Who Can" 5–6).

Sandy Asher, author of *A Woman Called Truth*, faced opposition to her work early on from "those who believe a white playwright should not be writing about a black character" and "actors [who] protested that they were being asked to play a role written by a white author" (Matetzschk-Campbell and Newman 68). Asher notes: "That sort of turmoil seems to have died down. I'm glad. I'd hate to be doomed to writing only about middle-aged, near-sighted, Jewish woman for audiences of middle-aged, near-sighted, Jewish women. I do believe human understanding and empathy can be stretched a bit further!" (as quoted in Matetzschk-Campbell and Newman 68–69).

It was against this complex and sometimes emotion-wrought backdrop that we asked respondents:

What advice would you give to a playwright who wanted to write from or about a cultural perspective that is not her or his own?

We found that responses largely fell into two categories: some argued about whether such cross-cultural writing was appropriate to begin with (raising points similar and complementary to those from Schroeder-Arce's article), while others offered practical advice on how playwrights ought to approach such writing if they were going to take on a project of that nature. As such, we present the responses to these two sub-questions separately.

Question A: Should/can a playwright write from or about cultural perspectives that are not her or his own?

José Casas

"As I look at the landscape of this field, I feel that diversity is an issue that still needs to be discussed in an honest fashion. When I look at seasons, I see more of a need for writers of color. I feel that this field needs to give opportunities to writers who are trying to tell the stories of their communities, histories, and experiences. These plays need to be produced and promoted on a larger scale. Many times, I have seen these stories written by playwrights who are not from those communities and I feel there is an imbalance that needs to be addressed. However, that doesn't mean I am advocating playwrights don't tell those stories.

Regardless of whether it is an adult play or a play designed for youth, I would never censor any artist from creating the art they wish to create. At times, I feel that writers that write about communities other than their own have been exploitive, but I also believe that a number of these playwrights come from a place of appreciation, love, and creative exploration."

Larissa FastHorse

"Since I am a half Native American and half white playwright, I advocate for the freedom to tell any story. I don't want to be limited to stories about half-breed NDNs from South Dakota who become ballet dancers that retire to a life of writing. I'm already commissioned to write that story […] but if that is all I am allowed to write, I'm going to have a short career. However, I want to add an amendment. You can tell any story, but if you choose to write about a specific Native American culture, take the time to represent them accurately" ("Who Should" para. 1).

Emily Freeman

"I believe that specificity is incredibly important when writing stories that address identity, social justice topics, values, or belief systems. The TYA canon should continue to expand to address stories that reflect the diversity of our audiences. Representation is a powerful tool for shifting the status quo and dominant narratives that oppress and generate otherness. But I also think playwrights should be cautious. Plays can easily become overly generalized, excluding the audiences that the playwright was attempting to reach initially. Instead, specificity invites our diverse audiences to find connections across race, identity, socioeconomic status, gender, etc. Focus on specific experiences, stories, or characters and connections will be drawn by the audience."

José Cruz González

"Most of my work focuses on the Latino community. This is an underserved community that is hungry for stories that reflect their reality. There's a handful of us working trying to reach that audience. I hope more playwrights will reach out to these underserved communities."

Beth Murray

"Nothing is neutral. Even writing another play that is safely similar to 800 plays preceding it is an ideologically charged act. It is an act that in the eyes of some honors tradition while in the eyes of others stagnates at the status quo, with a dozen variations on the continuum between. While some see challenging subject matter as the site of ideological charge, for me, the really pressing ideological challenges linger in the realm of cultural borders and representation which can mean subject matter, or it can simply mean whose story is being told, by whom, to whom, how, and for what purpose. We are a white-English-speaking-middle-class-female-straight dominated field. We are accustomed to seeing ourselves on the

margins. We don't think of ourselves as oppressive, yet we are awash in invisible habits that perpetuate intractability, until we ask difficult questions. Every story does not belong to every playwright. The way a playwright earns the trust to write across a cultural border is important, for sometimes in seeking that trust, the playwright discovers the story is not his or hers to tell – or to tell alone."

Lisa Portes

"I hope that all writers for young audiences pay attention to the way the world looks to American children now. It is vastly different than it looked even a generation ago. I also hope that writers seek to reflect onstage as many different kinds of people as possible, because the audience is filled with many different kinds of people. When a child sees herself reflected onstage it tells her that she matters. TYA is one of the last bastions of truly populist theatre because it generally isn't dependent on the single ticket buyer who has the socio-economic capacity to purchase the ticket. Often schools are buying the tickets and in many cases theatres are able to subsidize tickets in order to encourage attendance by children of all backgrounds. TYA provides a golden *opportunity for writers to create work that is relevant to and reflective of the huge and beautiful circle of people that make up the United States in the twenty-first century."*

Roxanne Schroeder-Arce

"I have engaged with the question of who can tell what story for many years and in many ways, as a scholar and practitioner. As a white playwright who primarily writes plays with US Latino/a and Latin American themes, stories, and characters, I am almost always working across identity markers. I do not take on this task lightly. I also don't feel prepared to write about any given culture. I live in a bicultural, bilingual world. Most of my closest family members are Mexican Americans living in a bicultural, bilingual world. While that is true, it is also true that I did not grow up in a Latino home, so I am not a native to Latino cultures. I am aware of the potential for my work to be or be perceived as appropriation, but I do not feel that inhibits me from writing. I write what I am compelled to write, the stories that come to me and ask for me to tell them. As I write, I do not question what I have a right to tell. Later, when I am in a critical space is when I (or others who choose to produce my plays or not) may ask those questions about my right to tell the stories I do.

My playwriting mentor, Suzan Zeder, once said that a playwright cannot be both artist and critic at the same time. That for me extends to the characters and stories I write about. However, I have to keep coming back to this question. That is one responsibility that comes with my privileged skin. I also am aware that there are not enough Latino/a voices on our stages. I feel that writing the plays that I do potentially leads to more Latino/a actors finding work and more Latino/a children seeing stories and people they recognize onstage. I hope to be offering more in this area rather than taking away, and I feel I am doing that. But, I have to keep asking that question. I would advise everyone working across identity markers to do that. Also, one needs to be aware of what else is there and who else is there ready to tell the stories. I try to advocate for Latino/a voices as often as I can yet Latino stories come to me, asking to be told."

Question B: How might a playwright best go about writing from or about cultural perspectives that are not her or his own?

José Casas

"One must go beyond what is expected. One must do extensive research for that community but, even more so, a playwright must gain an understanding of the community that they might not have had before. They need to talk to people in those communities. They need to understand how a community might react to their work because the images presented on those stages won't reflect the author. They must write universal stories that do not dilute the specifics of the community they are writing about. Finally, playwrights must be able to respond to any questions that community will [and should] have toward their individual work and inspirations. There is a fine line between cultural appreciation and cultural appropriation and a playwright needs to be able to understand that."

Larissa Fasthorse

"Take the time to represent [the culture] accurately. [...] Doing this will mean extra time and work. I do not mean reading a bunch of articles or books by non-members of that tribe. Then you are simply repeating information from another outsider's point of view, information coming through a cultural filter that has nothing to do with the people you want to write about. You have to actually contact the specific tribe. You laugh at how obvious this is, but trust me, it is rarely done. Or is lamely attempted, with scant consideration for cultural differences that require adjusting your approach and timeline. Native American tribes are sovereign nations with separate languages and cultures that are very different from the mainstream and each other. This is why you want to write about them, so be patient and do your work" ("Who Should" para. 2).

Dennis Foon

"Research and interview. Read as much as you can about the culture and spend as much time interviewing people from that culture as possible. And once you have a decent draft, get people from that culture with whom you have a good rapport to critique what you've written. And listen carefully to what they say. There are always many universals that writers can draw on to create credible characters from a wide range of backgrounds. But once you become specific, it's the details that become crucial."

Emily Freeman

"Acknowledging one's own identity and privilege is essential. Engage the community in your writing process if possible. If you are writing a play or characters that exist outside of your own experiences and identity, ask for help. Create a writing group or cohort of people to help you explore ideas and check your privilege if it becomes problematic."

Joanna Kraus

"Do your homework. When I was working on The Ice Wolf *(based on an Inuit print) I did extensive research both in Canada and in university libraries. I read explorer's descriptions of the frozen north and searched for appropriate names, ceremonies, superstitions, and legends. When I'd done a few drafts I sought out a specialist in Inuit culture to catch any errors I might have made. Later, when I was commissioned to write a play on North Carolina history, which became* Sunday Gold, *I read several books on state history. Once I'd settled on my topic I visited the old mining town of Gold Hill, even panned for gold myself, consulted countless documents related to working in the mines and living in that area at the time; e.g., who were the rocker girls, what were contemporary family values, attitudes, and prejudices of the time, etc. Absolutely everything had to be approved by the North Carolina Museum of History before going into rehearsal, and I went back to revise several times."*

Psalmayene 24

"My advice would be for the playwright to dig into the material (or main character) until they find the universal human core that binds us all. This is much easier said than done. When I was writing the last play in my Hip-Hop Children's Trilogy, Cinderella: The Remix, *I was initially apprehensive because I had never written a play with a female protagonist. I wanted the voice to be authentic, and not sound like a man writing a girl character. It was challenging, but during the process of writing the play, I was able to confront uncomfortable truths within myself and eventually connect with the heart and soul of my Cinderella character. Only after this process was I able to write freely. In my opinion, playwrights' willingness to be vulnerable and their ability to approach and inhabit the different cultural perspectives with honesty, sensitivity, and respect are crucial if they are going to write a play that rises above flat, offensive stereotypes."*

Roxanne Schroeder-Arce

"As a playwright, I think about the story that is being told. As I write bilingual plays, for example, I write in Spanish when the character needs to speak in Spanish, and English when the character needs to speak in English. I don't sit with a meter deciding that it's now time for one or the other language. It's also not about access. It's about the character sharing at any given time in the way s/he speaks. I was asked to put some of the songs in my play Mariachi Girl *into English to make it more accessible to English speakers. Along with the*

composer, Héctor Martinez Morales, I tried, but it was not possible. The Spanish language was critical to the music, moment, and characters. Sometimes a window or authentic glance that asks us to feel another culture is more important than understanding everything we see and hear. Also, inviting dominant cultures to lean in is healthy for everyone."

Y York

"You have an obligation to research and listen to this culture that is calling to you. Be careful of stereotype; you can avoid stereotype by knowing the reason and source for each character trait that you employ. Make sure you can stand behind your work, and then be brave about it. Listen carefully to your critics as they may reveal some truth. Learning goes on until we're dead."

Suzan Zeder

"As playwrights it is not our job to be the voice of any cultural perspective, our own or anyone else's. It is our job to create characters with as much depth, compassion, clarity, specificity, and complexity as possible; to weave plots from stories made of action not polemics, to explore themes that take us into dark and unknown places inside ourselves and others. If these reflect a particular "cultural" heritage that we have ourselves, well and good, but do not let that be a limitation. No one owns a culture, not even those who share it by birthright.

What you must *do, writing about any culture, even one you think you may know from direct experience, is to explore it as if it were an unknown territory. You must literally fill yourself with information, history, sights, sounds, song, longings, dream, wishes, and lies about whoever and whatever you are writing about. Where we can get into trouble as playwrights writing outside the margins of our own "culture" or experience is when we presume to speak "for it." That is both arrogance and assumption. But if we approach our own or any culture from a position of respectful ignorance and allow the characters, situations, themes, issues, conflicts, and resolutions to educate us enough to give voice to characters who will speak for themselves, I think we avoid the pitfall."*

Taboos and controversial issues

An ongoing debate in contemporary America asks: what is appropriate for young people? This question is applied to theatre, film, television, video games, and other media. People strongly disagree about what is appropriate to share with young people in each context. This is an especially complex question, given that people's feelings about what is appropriate (in various types of theatre for people of different ages) are guided by contextual factors; as van de Water notes, people's views of "appropriateness" are "both culturally determined and subject to changing views of children and childhood" (61).

Beth Murray explains: "Doing anything for or with children as an adult" involves an "admirable adult urge 'to protect' young people [that] is open to wide interpretation. At one extreme, it involves exposing children to strategic pushes and challenges and encounters with fear and danger trusting them to make sense for themselves. At another extreme, it involves shielding children from anything that may hurt, cause discomfort, or feel dangerous/scary."

Both ends of this spectrum were addressed in a survey of 332 individuals invested in TYA, including artists, K-12 educators, funding agencies, and university TYA specialists. Seventy-nine percent of respondents indicated that "TYA should not shy away from addressing particular topics" even if they might be controversial, while only 11% indicated "there were topics the field should definitely or probably avoid"; 7% indicated it depended on contextual factors and 3% gave other responses (Omasta "Adult" 78). While the majority of participants felt all topics could be addressed, those who felt particular topics should be avoided most frequently mentioned sex (n=19) and violence (n=9) (79). Perhaps unsurprisingly, some 90 years earlier Montrose Moses noted: "I can see only one phrase where [TYA artists] would have to be careful not to go beyond childhood in dealing with emotional: sex" (607).

On the other hand, when asked if "TYA companies have a responsibility to address social issues in at least some of their programming," 64% of respondents indicated they did, while 23% indicated they did not (Omasta "Adult" 82). By far the most common issue participants indicated should be addressed was bullying (n=64), followed by race/racism (n=45); other issues related to diversity and discrimination were frequently mentioned (83). In sum, the majority of participants (despite a significant minority) felt that TYA should not refrain from engaging with controversial issues and, in many participants' views, ought to do so.

The debate over appropriate material for children is hardly new. It can be traced from Plato's *Republic* through the eighteenth century writings of figures like Stephani de Genlis (France), Hannah More (England), and Charles Stearns (USA). It continued to be debated through in American Settlement Houses, productions presented by the Junior League of America, and so on through the present. Writing in 1967, Birner called for TYA to move away from the saccharine in favor of addressing real issues, arguing: "For many years there was an unwritten lay that satire for children was forbidden, [...] but the real world is not all sweetness and light. It is bitterness and darkness too, and a repertoire that aims to hold the mirror up to nature must reflect all of nature's hues" (xvi).

Pearson-Davis agrees that "until the 1960's playwrights and producers for young audiences not only avoided depth of characterization, but they also stayed away from contemporary subject matter and controversial themes. They did not want to alienate parents and teachers during a time period when very narrow limits were set on what was considered appropriate for children" (xvii). But in the later decade of the twentieth century playwrights and producers began to introduce more complex themes into their work. As Goldberg observes: "There would be no Huck Finn without prejudice, no Jim Hawkins without greed, and no Snow White without jealousy. Those who would remove examples of evil from the child's view must necessarily also remove examples of those who defeat evil. Alas, he will see the evil anyway – in life. The active defeat of evil he is less likely to run across" (*Children's* 125).

This view that young people must see villains in order to see heroes evolved over time as playwrights began to argue that young people needed to see not just adult heroes, but to face a real world that can be dark and complex, sometimes without heroes. Smith notes that "the world can be a scary place and theatre that tries to deny that doesn't really help. [...] Yes, there are frightening things out there but watching young people on stage working through them, learning how to cope with them through love, courage and honesty can only help prepare our new generations for the world we're leaving them" (Smith 1997, x). The view that young audiences watching other young people solve their own problems led to the emergence of genuine child protagonists in the late 1970s. Some of the most well-known examples of these include Suzan Zeder's Ellie from *Step on a Crack* and Wiley from *Wiley and the Hairy Man*.

As the survey results above suggest, the paradigm that real young people need to experience real characters in the theatre continues to resonate today. As Zacarías notes: "Theatre offers an entertainment, an escape. But at the same time, it really needs to [offer] tools for kids to deal with the real world. [...] We want our kids to see plays that make them unafraid to deal with issues that kids talk about a lot" (as quoted in van Kerckhove 34). And perhaps, as Finegan Kruckmeyer suggests, it is by presenting young people with plays in which they experience difficult emotions like sadness, and only in those situations, that "*they are truly the protagonist*. They are not necessarily heroes yet (just for having been abandoned), but if a hero were to emerge, it would surely be them" (para. 8, original emphasis).

All these factors considered, we asked respondents:

How can playwrights approach writing scripts that explore territory likely to be considered "controversial"?

Laurie Brooks

"If you know (or suspect) your play will raise some controversy it's okay to be worried or even afraid but don't let that stop you. If the work lives in the authentic world of young adults, if you've done your homework and if you truly care about issues that challenge young adults, that's what's important. You must be willing to write a play that will be difficult to produce. When I wrote The Wrestling Season, *I thought no one would get it, like it, or produce it. I wrote it because I cared deeply about the ideas and characters and was driven to write the story. When that passion is present, trust it. The road may be long but it will be worth the journey. Disclose, disclose, disclose. When presenting a play with challenging issues, it is crucial to reveal any content that may be controversial. Do not be apologetic. Believe in the quality and worth of the work."*

Matt Buchanan

"I do not say to shy away from 'issues' like divorce. I personally have very little patience with those who feel that 'sensitive' topics must always be avoided when writing for kids. Properly handled, issues of sex, death, disease, war, etc. can make for very powerful art with young people – though there may be financial concerns here – if you go too controversial you'll lose out on the more conservative part of the market."

José Casas

"In terms of work that is, usually, ideologically charged, I honestly believe that artists should proceed as they would in any other situation. I love the fact that youth are so honest about what they see. However, I do believe that it is very important to understand the age group a playwright is attempting to target. Personally, I tend to think that children are resilient and, depending on the story, can be exposed to issues other adults might not think are appropriate. In the end, this issue becomes a negotiation between theatre and playwright, playwright and audiences. I think each story and subsequent production has to come to an agreement in regards to how they feel about the expected audience reactions; not only from youth but, in many cases, the parents and/or academic institutions."

Maggie-Kate Coleman

"As a Youth Theatre educator, I ran a musical theatre program spanning the ages of 11–17 for many years. Though we occasionally encountered some pushback over the material we were giving them – songs and scenes from a wide range of the musical theatre oeuvre, we found year after year that students consistently responded in an overwhelmingly positive manner to material that we had been told was 'too complex' for youth. I learned so much from working with these students: they were hungry for new work that spoke to their experience, they connected to work that addressed difficult topics, like depression, suicide, disillusionment with society, culture, government, and values. And without prompt or design on our part, they consistently used the work as a jumping off point to engage in dialogue with us and each other about their own lives."

Debbie Devine

Because American TYA companies are reluctant to take on complex issues, *"playwrights, actors, directors and designers see family programming as second rate, second class and refuse to do it and perpetuate the bad work that is 80% of what is being produced in the United States. Europe, South America, Canada, and so much of the rest of the world are way ahead of us on the courage of content. They know children are resilient humans and need to be challenged."*

Emily Freeman

"As TYA playwrights, we must actively choose whether audience drives the story, or, more importantly, whether gatekeepers drive the story. Some playwrights write dual narratives, one

for the young audience members and one for the adults. I try to write integrated plays with stories and dialogue that don't exclude particular audience members based on their experience level or age. Yet, when you know a story will create controversy, what do you do?

My advice is to go for it! Before you stop yourself from writing a story because of its potential to be produced or not, write it! Once you have the script completed, you may have to take on new roles, such as producer, marketing manager, or even activist, but it is worth it. Our audiences deserve diverse languages, identities, bodies, and stories in the canon. Additionally, you can't predict outcomes. People may surprise you and controversy may lead to unexpected and extraordinary social change."

Dwayne Hartford

"Controversial issues, by nature, make for good drama. If you are passionate about a particular issue, and you feel like you have something to say that will resonate with young audiences, go for it. Just know going in that the play may have a hard time finding a production. Producing theatres have to sell seats, and they know their communities. Some are more willing and/or able to push their audiences than others, and some communities are more open to challenging subjects than others. Just write a good play. Tell a good story. Then, get that script in the hands of a brave artistic director. For myself, the only hard rule is that I must leave my audience with possibilities, with hope."

Madeleine L'engle

"The writer whose words are going to be read by children has a heavy responsibility. And yet, despite the undeniable fact that the children's minds are tender, they are also far more tough than many people realize, and they have an openness and an ability to grapple with difficult concepts which many adults have lost" (as quoted by Kilpatrick).

Mark Lutwak

"Don't assume you know what will be controversial. Institutions that produce theatre vary. While a larger children's theatre may shy away from work dealing with gender, sexuality, or family violence (for example), a smaller theatre may hunger for that material. Certain health and social action groups that specialize in working with those issues have a different relationship with schools than the 'flagship' company in the same community."

Bob Moss

"People do like to see plays that reflect their own lives, and playwrights are sometimes compelled to write about their own experiences. Good. We can and should have all kinds of theatrical opportunities. If someone is writing for a particular market, then perhaps some societal concerns might manifest themselves. The Hangar Theatre in Ithaca, NY recently commissioned a play about a young man coming out in high school. Ithaca is an extremely liberal community, but a few schools opted out. Most took the play, and had wonderful talk-backs with it."

Beth Murray

"For those playwrights hoping to push against the well-intentioned censorship of grown-ups mediating theatre for young audiences, the most successful break-throughs seem to come in small, targeted, artistic projects whose impact creates a ripple of risk that makes it safe for others to ride. Some of the most impactful efforts emerge at the most seemingly intractable crossroads. Before Oily Cart, we didn't think about 'special needs' and 'differing abilities' as being a welcomed, central part of the aesthetic of a piece. Before Laurie Brooks's The Wrestling Season *and Suzan Zeder's* Doors, *teen LGBTQ identity and divorce were taboo topics. Before José Cruz González writing up and down the bilingual/bicultural spectrum, mainstream TYA theatres were largely monolingual.*

If it is in your heart and your work to conquer some barrier, push artistically, protect children responsively, collaborate in the community beyond theatre, remain respectfully aware of 'detractors' as 'concerned adults,' and respond through shared concern for young people, find insider allies to educate and let them educate you, too – their voice is frequently more trusted than yours. Good art takes a risk and pushes people. We are obligated to do that, but there is a balance to strike in TYA because the combination of censors and soap boxes can become myopic and destructive – on both sides – to the art and the children's experience. It's frequently about so much more than the play."

Jonathan Rand

"In many cases, less is more. Sometimes you can sneak in a jab without being so overt that the show gets canceled before it begins. Besides, it's more challenging and ultimately more satisfying to coat a poison pill with chocolate and see who figures it out."

Adults writing for and about children

Many regard the works of Shakespeare and some of the Ancient Greek playwrights as among the finest pieces of dramatic literature. Nevertheless, these collected plays (like most from their epochs) share a common feature: everyone associated with their production (the authors, sponsors/producers, actors, etc.) were all men. While they may collectively contain strong female characters women's roles, the systematic exclusion of women from having any part in developing or performing the works no doubt led to stereotyping and other troubles. As Sue-Ellen Case (1988) observes: "it is important to remember that the notion of the female derived from the male point of view, which remained alien to female experience and reflected the perspective of the gendered opposite" (11). While any given male playwright may certainly be able to write a complex and realistic female character role, when the canon of plays from an entire era is written *exclusively* by men, problems arise.

While it would be clearly problematic if the field of theatre determined that only men were able to write roles for women, or only Caucasian playwrights were allowed to write roles for black or Latino characters, we pay little attention to the fact that – by and large – only adults write child characters (both in terms of TYA, where young actors are performed for audiences of young people, and in Youth Theatre, where young people themselves perform). There are of course exceptions to this rule; *The Fifty-Second Street Project* (and its sister programs across the US) engages youth in writing plays that are performed by adults. Applied Theatre programs (both professional and amateur) involve young people in the process of writing plays they will eventually perform. Yet, by and large, adults author the overwhelming majority of published scripts in TYA and Youth Theatre. Whether or not this is a problem depends on one's perspective on if children constitute a social class (as scholars such as Lee have in earlier chapters). If one agrees with Lee, this could be seen as akin to a situation where only white authors write black characters.

Some might respond that this case is different because "we were all children once." This begs the question: is what it means to be a child today at all similar to what it meant to be a child when today's adults were young? Is it different to be a child in a post-9/11 world, where school shootings are frequent across the nation, and where school time beginning in elementary school is dominated by preparing for high-stakes standardized testing? While adults may indeed share experiences with children (and with all humanity), it seems unlikely that adult playwrights can fully understand the lives of young people, even if they have children themselves. Time creates distances, memory fades and even creates false recollections, and it becomes difficult to distinguish what *was* from one's *perception* of what was. This does not mean that adults should not write stories for young people, only that they should be cognizant that they are writing for/about an audience they may not completely understand.

Playwrights' careful attention to this matter will be helpful to the directors and actors who will ultimately bring a play to life before an audience. When asked about the ethical ramifications of adult artists working with/for young people, most spoke about issues surrounding age-appropriate casting, but their responses can also provide insights to playwrights.

What are the ethical ramifications of adults writing plays for youth that will typically be directed by adults and in which adults may perform the roles of children/youth?

Megan Alrutz

"Young people bring a particular set of valuable skills, wisdom, and experiences to theatre and so do the trained adult artists who work with them. I don't believe that everyone should write, direct, or perform for young people. However, adults who understand how to create theatre as a youth-ally – someone working with/for young people to achieve some of their goals/desires – have an opportunity to use their own training and wisdom in the service of young audiences."

Jeannine Coulombe

"*We are a very child-centric theatre. We train youth performers. We cast youth performers. Our audiences have more youth present than adults. Our main rule of thumb is: If the character is a child, it is played by a child. If the character is an adult, it is played by an adult. As a basic guideline, 80–90% of the roles in our productions are played by youth actors and 10–20% are played by adult mentor actors. We find something extremely powerful in youth actors telling stories to youth audiences. It is magical. It's what we do. There is an authenticity and a level of communication that occurs between youth performers and youth audiences that cannot be replicated by adults playing those roles.*"

Julia Flood

"*We deal with age-appropriate casting on a case by case basis when approaching a play. Sometimes the decision is largely practical – for example, an extensive tour into schools is not possible for a school-aged child actor. Often casting a 22-year-old who looks 14 is simply a matter of casting the most skilled actor for the job. At times, though, when the age of the character is really central to the artistic integrity of the production, we make the choice to take on the added rehearsal time, training, and care that working responsibly with child actors requires. It comes down to storytelling and respect for our artists, whether child or adult. How can we best tell this story and what will it require of us to do so?*"

Stephen Fredericks

"*We do this on a per piece basis. I generally prefer to work with age appropriate casting, but shows that are performed during the week for schools in addition to our weekend Main Stage productions require us to utilize an all-adult cast. I also believe that the playwright should be a part of the discussion so that you retain your responsibility to their original vision.*"

Tamara Goldbogen

"*As a director working primarily with college-age actors on theatre for young audience scripts I start every production with inner child work. I lead actors through a series of activities that I borrow from the book* Spaces of Creation *written by Suzan Zeder and Jim Hancock. Asking adult actors to actively and intentionally connect with their inner child has been instrumental in my process and in working to inspire authentic performances by adults portraying young people onstage.*"

Jeffrey Revels

"*I do not have any concerns with young adults playing children. The story or script will determine if our company will go with young adults or with children playing the roles. We do both. It depends on the story and the director. If we are having young adults playing children, I try to match a director with the show that has a grasp on directing the young adults in effective ways to play a child, which is basically to play an honest character and stay away from adopting a series of physical tics and speech patterns that somehow we as adults seem to think telegraph that we are 'playing a child'. There is a big difference between childlike and childish. We aim for childlike."*

David Wood

"When it comes to the playing of child characters, rules and regulations often affect professional companies. The solution, often, is to have the role played by a young actor, say in his or her early twenties, who looks young enough to be reasonably convincing in the role. Furthermore, if the child in the story plays a major role, and is really the 'motor' of the play, it would be folly to employ a child of say, ten years of age, to play the part onstage over a season of performances. A child could not be expected to sustain such a performance, driving through the story efficiently and accurately, every single performance. Even if the law allowed the child to do every performance I think it would be a mistake.

Over the years I have used many young actors in different plays. Sophie in The BFG *has always been played by an adult actress. When I directed my adaptation of Dahl's* The Witches, *I searched in vain for a young actor to play Boy. The problem was that everyone who auditioned had, naturally, a voice that had broken! The dialogue just didn't sound right. The solution was to find a remarkable female actor, who did a wonderful job. Most of the children in the audience never questioned the fact that the boy wasn't a boy!*

The one big exception to the rule was in my adaptation of Michelle Magorian's Goodnight Mister Tom, *in which the vulnerability of the evacuee, Willie, who has been cruelly treated by his mother, meant that we really needed a child to play the part. This affected my adaptation, in that I made sure that we were not simply looking at the story through the child's eyes, making him the main driving force of the play. This role is carried by Mister Tom, the elderly recluse who is forced to accommodate the child in his cottage in the country, when Willie arrives from London. The decision was unquestionably the right one, even though it meant having three young boys playing Willie, rotating week by week throughout the West End season and tour. All the logistical problems this created, plus the expense of having chaperones and tutors, paid off – the production managed to win an Olivier Award."*

Stephani Etheridge Woodson

"For one, youth are furthered from the production process. Adults are not children. We are always other. Representational ethics will always be important then. There is of course no 'truth' nor should we imagine realism and realistic to be the same. It is important adults acknowledge their difference and make art for and of the now, rather than filled with nostalgic longing for what kids should be or how they 'remember' childhood."

***

Ultimately, ideology and ethics are both shared and deeply personal. This chapter has presented a wide range of passionate and often contradictory views regarding representation, cross-cultural writing, addressing controversial or taboo topics, and more. In this area perhaps more than others, there are no "right answers." All playwrights must navigate their personal values and decide what they are comfortable addressing, how they want to do so, and what they believe is most important to share with the world. The only thing we believe is certain is that all writing is always ideological – everything (from the adaptation of a well-known fairy tale to an original work exploring issues at the forefront of contemporary politics) is deeply laden with messages intended and otherwise, and we encourage writers to be highly cognizant of what precisely their work is saying to audiences.

Chapter 4

Practical Considerations

Confronting the blank page may be daunting, exciting, or fall somewhere in between. A playwright might prefer to write his initial script alone, or enjoy creating his script with collaborators. However a playwright approaches generating new material, being aware of some of the practical considerations of writing TYA before getting started can provide him with a great array of useful tools and keep him from feeling out of his element. We asked our respondents a number of questions about their experiences and perspectives on dealing with specific practical concerns of conceiving, writing, and working with new TVY scripts.

In our last chapter, we explored ethical considerations. Many of these practical considerations build on framing one's initial thinking and avoiding certain pitfalls and errors. One could think of chapter three as priming a building site (the artist's mind), and this chapter as an exploration of method (playwrights' tools, materials, and structures).

While there are similarities between writing original work and adapting from other sources, the numerous differences led us to dedicate the next chapter to a discussion of both the artistic and business/legal concerns regarding adaptation. Nevertheless, many of the principles from this and other chapters can be applied to adaptations, so we also encourage readers to review these, rather than skipping directly to chapter five, which assumes readers are already familiar with the content in these earlier chapters. Furthermore, whether a playwright writes alone or collaboratively, for clarity and ease of address we refer to the writer as an individual.

Finally, while this chapter focuses on practical considerations before and during the process of writing a TYA play, as well as concluding with some thoughts about what to do with a draft once it is completed, if readers are looking for *writing exercises* (for general and/or youth audiences), they may visit Appendix A for additional texts and resources.

Understanding young people's perspectives

In the previous chapter we discussed the challenges of entering another culture in order to write out of appreciation rather than appropriation, and introduced perspectives that view childhood as a unique culture. Goldberg describes how watching young people reveals eye-opening differences: "There seem to be definitive patterns of behavior, seldom revealed in adults, which erupt freely from children, particularly in groups" (*Children's* 128). In that context, as many of our respondents advised, a writer should do his homework. Susman-Stillman argues that this work is imperative:

> Knowing how children grow and change, and what they are capable of knowing, doing, and understanding, is critical to introducing theatre arts and its skills to young children and to creating work that appropriately matches and scaffolds their creative, cognitive, and social development.

(vii)

While it may seem obvious that actively seeking to understand young people is crucial for any playwright who wants to write about or for them, not every playwright does; even if they do, it is not always clear how best to pursue this knowledge. We therefore asked respondents to share practical approaches and perspectives on this matter. Many responses relate to the importance of diving into child culture by getting to know young people as individuals, thereby moving beyond potential stereotyping and misconceptions in one's work.

How can adults get in touch with genuine child perspectives?

Janet Allen

> "As naïve as it sounds, I think playwrights writing for kids need to hang out with them – not just read about them, or read what they read, but hang out with them. Learning from parents and teachers is great, but hanging out with kids when they are playing in an unstructured way, and talking to kids about what matters to them outside of a school setting is a really valuable experience."

Laurie Brooks

> "Young adults have a real sense for anything that is inauthentic or patronizing. And if they sense it they will not be kind. Best to spend some quality time with young people the age your play targets. Don't be afraid to ask questions. Young people make terrific advisors for TYA playwrights."

Dwayne Hartford

> "Talking with young people is invaluable. Ask a child to tell you a story."

Samantha Macher

> "I think one of my biggest sources for any of my plays is by meeting and interacting with the people that I hope to write for. I've had the opportunity to teach writing workshops for teens and middle-graders. When I get these opportunities, I just try to listen to them and see what

themes appear in their conversations, or what concerns are in the forefront of their minds. Then, and only if I feel like I'm able to write well on those topics, I take a stab at writing a play that I think might be relevant to them. I think that writing TYA is in many ways like writing for adult audiences: It's about finding a universal story and making it specific."

Anne Negri

"With young people I find it helpful to know the performers before I write for/with them. I may choose a theme or setting for the play at the outset, but I find that workshopping, improvising, devising, and teaching that group of performers is a major part of writing something they will enjoy performing. With middle-school students I tend to write comedies. Comedies tend to fall within their emotional wheelhouse at their age and they relish the opportunity to be in the spotlight and get laughs from the audience. I often write an initial or basic draft and then I bring it to my students. I enter the rehearsal process with very little ego about my writing. I tell my students that we can change/cut/add anything, as long as it is school-appropriate and makes sense for the logic of the story. Some students prefer to stick to my words verbatim and others embrace the openness of the script and they come up with original ideas that are far more creative than what I initially wrote."

Greg Romero

"I think I've gained the most by just listening to what stories young people are themselves telling. I had the privilege of working a couple times with a program called The Mantua Project, in which young writers (ages 8–13) from the Mantua neighborhood of West Philadelphia wrote short plays over the course of a weekend, which later went into production. Their plays were some of the most thrilling, dynamic, honest, theatrical plays I had seen or read in years. I think it was because they were fully expressing their wonderful imaginations, free from expectations (road-blocks) of what a play should be. Their plays had lots of non-human characters going on impossible, necessary journeys, endless action, and some of the most imaginative visual information you could dream up. These kinds of experiences, as well as just having conversations or co-imagining with young people have given me all the guidance I need to understand what stories might interest young audiences."

Roxanne Schroeder-Arce

"One thing I do is I watch children all the time, not to write a play, but because I am fascinated by young people. I often ask my eight-year-old to read my words and tell me if they ring true to her. She readily tells me her honest thoughts!"

***

While artists and theorists may investigate potential differences in child culture and perspective, others (and perhaps even the same artists and theorists) may also explore similarities between young people and adults. Zacarías speaks to the universality of some elements of the human experience: "[…] both children and adults want the same big things: love, recognition, and revenge. It is only the journey that is seasoned by the age, experience, and particular details of the character" (para. 16). Suzan Zeder cautions playwrights against making any assumptions about children and youth as a separate culture:

> I believe that the minute you start categorizing your audience, they become the "other." You will make assumptions that are dangerous, there is no such thing as a "typical" 10 year old. Some are goofy as loons and others are wise beyond all reckoning. To write "for" any particular target while it focuses the work becomes exclusive in excluding all those you are *not* writing *for*.

Furthermore, Zeder reflects upon the perceived separation of childhood from adulthood:

> I really don't think of my childhood as something in the distant past. I'm becoming more and more convinced that within us is the child that we always are. Not always were, but always *are*. Conversely, I think we have within us, as children, the men and women we become.

Besides considering genuine child/youth (and universal) perspectives, if a writer wants to work on TYA scripts, it is also helpful to know what TYA plays already exist. Playwrights should investigate what plays get produced, to what audiences those plays are exposed, and how those audiences receive the work. As Goldberg notes: "The successful playwright is usually one who has watched a lot of young audiences responding to a variety of stage events" (*Children's* 130–131). It may also be instructive for a playwright to read as many scripts as possible.

Here are some ways to find TYA scripts to read:

- Check the season listings (present and past) on TYA companies' websites or talk to local drama teachers to see what plays they are producing, and purchase scripts of those plays when available (Internet retailers often have published plays in stock).
- Read trade publications to keep up with what is trending (see Appendix A).
- Purchase collections/anthologies of works from well-known playwrights, or from particular theatre seasons or events, often frequently available for purchase online, or perhaps available from a library.
- Develop relationships with theatres, publishers, or organizers of TYA-related festivals or contests and volunteer as a reader. Many organizations receive numerous scripts and might be open to assistance.
- Attend conferences in the field, many of which present and/or sell new scripts in the field (see Appendices B and C).

Our respondents also had a number of other creative and practical suggestions when we asked:

What are some ways to get to know the market/canon of TYA literature?

Laurie Brooks

"Get out into the world of TYA. Pay attention to what people are doing, writing, and saying. Meet people. Don't be shy. Let people know who you are. Network like crazy. Don't be shy to approach people in the field you admire. Listen carefully to those who have been in the trenches. And don't be afraid to ask for help! Most of us who have been around for a while are eager to help new talent."

José Cruz González

"I believe a playwright should take workshops or classes whenever possible. It is important to be in a community of playwrights. If there isn't one, create it yourself. Be proactive about your work. Create your own readings and workshops."

David Kilpatrick

"I would suggest they ask to be in the room, even as silent observer, of a developmental workshop of a piece. Practical experience is important, so finding ways to be in the room – in whatever capacity that may be – is helpful. Don't discount the importance of informational meetings with other TYA playwrights, TYA directors, and artistic directors of companies that produce work for young audiences."

Beth Murray

"A class in TYA is always helpful. Many include components on playwriting for young audiences. Short of that, a class in playwriting or children's literature or simply joining a playwriting group may be all the help someone needs to get inspired and started. Similarly inspiring is seeing plays for young audiences and paying as much attention to the audience as to the action onstage, then reading the script for comparison to see how the playwright's hand and the director's touch worked together, or not. It is wise for a playwright to frequently work in the support of others' plays (e.g., as an actor for a concert reading, as a member of a respondent audience, as a dramaturg, etc.). We learn different things in different ways when supporting another writer's work. Yet, the insights map onto our own writing worlds as well.

Dorothy Webb

"The best resource for playwrights is seeing plays – all kinds of plays, not necessarily TYA. Think about what you've seen. What moved you? Interested you? Read plays – all kinds of plays including good plays designed for young audiences. Read all of the plays of notable playwrights for young people. What did you learn about the various ways they structured their plays? About the ways they develop character and the ways they have their characters *make discoveries, the ways they moved the action. The point is to come to an understanding of their different approaches and the devices they use to accomplish those approaches. Go to workshops devoted to new plays. Listen to the readings; see how different playwrights approach their craft.*

***

In addition to getting to know young people personally and doing one's own research into the TYA market, there are limitless other ways to understand young people and their interests. Some sources Pam Sterling uses to inspire students include: "essays on children's literature; articles on the value of myths, dreams and fairy tales in contemporary drama; and chapters from Joseph Campbell, Bruno Bettleheim, and from Roger Sale's book *Fairytales and After.*" Many theatre artists find children's and YA literature a fantastic source for ideas and inspiration. As Greg Romero notes, "there are literary works that continue to inspire me, and that I often return to when I get lost."

Besides literature and live theatre, there is the constantly evolving world of technology. Many young people are highly conversant in television, film, and professionally and user-generated online media. Practitioners have various perspectives regarding how (or whether) the pervasive nature of multimedia has and will affect audiences. Dennis Foon warns: "don't ignore other media. Our audience is enveloped by this invasion, it's become part of the vocabulary." Moses Goldberg contends that the essential nature of theatre will prevail over digital media, and is "confident that TYA will eventually realize that its strength is not in imitation but in the basic appeal of live theatre where the actor commands the empathy of the young viewer."

Some artists attempt to harness young people's digital fluency in ways that enhance the theatrical experience through the integration of technology into a play itself or through activities that take place outside the play proper. Brooks notes:

> In the time of Facebook, Twitter, texting, selfies, and instant information, audiences crave greater involvement in the theatre experience. They want to be more than spectators who are entertained and then sent home without ever having been a meaningful part of the experience. In short, they want to be makers and doers. They are bored with being assigned the limited role of watchers.

She describes her work developing interactive forums that take place immediately after productions of her plays, observing: "When a play [is] performed with an Interactive Forum, audiences [are] more engaged, applause [is] more enthusiastic and patrons [leave] the theatre continuing to dialogue about the play" (2).

We asked respondents their perspectives on the potential effects of media on TYA audiences. Each offers a unique perspective and/or practical advice regarding a playwright's approach to the effects of "media invasion."

Has technology changed audiences' expectations, ways of responding, and ability to sit still for lengths of time?

Susan Gurman

"With the proliferation of electronic hand-held devices, theatre stands out, along with books, as still providing a chance for young people to dream while still awake."

Celise Kalke

"Playwrights should remember that adapting other mediums for the stage requires a respect of theatrical dramaturgy. Good dramaturgy in service of adapting pop culture, even video games, requires a deep understanding of patrons 'in' on the reference and patrons experiencing the reference for the first time. Finally, often video games or movies are meant to be experienced passively. Live theatre, especially for kids, often has a spirit of play embedded in the story telling. Even if it is just a pause for an audience reaction."

Finegan Kruckemeyer

"I do feel that a child's awareness of, and perceived dependence on, technology has affected the making of TYA – not so much in how an audience chooses to receive a work, but rather in how many theatre-makers choose to present one. At our fingertips right now are screens and lights and illusions, which may take one's breath away. And once our fingertips have dulled to the feel of those illusions, once our breath has returned, then the next version will present itself – and seemingly ever onwards. The possibilities are endless, we are told. But the wonder for an audience, I believe, can end.

Because once we commit to a celebration of the means of delivery, rather than the product delivered, we start investing in a different way. It is hinged on a simple belief: When we watch a complex magic show, we look for the wires, the proof of its falsehood. But when we watch a simple story told, then we look for the allegory, the proof of its truth. One form invites us to be sceptics, and then tries to prove us wrong. The other encourages us to be believers, and then tries to prove us right."

Andy Manley

"I am not sure that we need to keep other media in mind. They can be an inspiration for shows – but so can anything. I sometimes refer to story points in books and techniques in films, but often these are theatrical to start with. I think we have a wealth of techniques and theatrical devices that we can use; often it's more that we are afraid to use them in case others think we have 'borrowed' them. I have a slightly different fear that these online and solitary things will rob us of the characters and social interactions that we rely on in theatre.

Watching someone doing their shopping on a computer is probably less interesting in a theatrical sense than watching someone interact with a shop assistant. White, a show I made for 2–4 year olds had an app made but for it. For me though it was a support to the show, a way of extending the theatre experience."

***

Taking steps to understand digital media and how young people interact with it may help playwrights create better, deeper, and more cogent theatre for contemporary audiences.

Audience considerations

Some writers new to the field may wonder what young audiences will or will not understand. They might wonder whether plots need to be simplified, made more accessible, or follow a linear structure; whether "advanced" language should be avoided for some age groups; or whether they should strive to write a play that educates their audience in some manner. Playwrights may have heard they should "keep it simple" when writing TYA. But what does this really mean? And it is true? In order to fully explore these sometimes deceptively complex issues, we asked several respondents for their views.

Do TYA plays need to avoid complex or non-traditional plots?

Maggie-Kate Coleman

"The biggest mistake I see writers make when writing for youth audiences is erring on the side of simplicity of ideas rather than simplicity of storytelling. The mistaken belief that the majority of your audience is less intelligent than you are and that you should write down so your audience will be able to 'get it.' Striving for clarity in your work and storytelling and communicating ideas clearly does not mean that you should also strive for a lack of complexity out of the completely bogus fear that youth audiences cannot handle complicated or difficult themes, stories, and ideas. I recently worked on a musical primarily targeted at girls aged 11–14 based on interviews with female climate scientists and their academic research. We found that even younger audience members responded positively to the piece and were easily able to grasp some of the complex ideas presented. We also found that in the few areas that we mistakenly 'dumbed it down' too much, the kids did not respond as positively. They felt that those moments were silly or stupid or for babies."

Dwayne Hartford

"I have found young audiences to be more than willing to go on a nonlinear journey."

David Kilpatrick

"One of the biggest mistakes [playwrights] can make is to suddenly not write as strong of a play simply because they're writing for young audiences and think they can't handle it. A

62

misstep that often occurs is when playwrights say 'I'm going to write a play for 7 year olds' or 'I'm going to write a play that teaches children to stay away from drugs.' Children are very smart, sophisticated audiences and they know, even before you do, whether your play is talking down to them or is trying to teach them something, and they check out immediately."

David Saar

"I love complexity of character and thought, because I think that young people are capable and deserving of more depth than they are often offered."

Do TYA plays need to avoid language that is "too advanced" for young people?

Jeannine Coulombe

"I firmly believe in using a wide-range, rich, sophisticated vocabulary woven into a script that gives context to meaning. How else are children supposed to learn the beauty of language? I don't 'dumb-down' my vocabulary for my own children, why would I do that for youth audiences? There is no reason to talk down to an audience, whether adult or youth. I would rather like for all of us to talk up, youth and adult alike. The age ranges for our plays are usually dictated by our source material. As to vulgar language, audience age specificity is imperative. As a basic tenet I don't see an excess of vulgar language to be necessary to relate or convey character to an older TYA audience. There are more fun, creative, and colorful ways to express meaning and character."

Julia Flood

"Young people are used to learning new vocabulary on a daily basis by gleaning meaning from context, situation, and character. We do them a disservice if we think that they cannot grasp advanced language or complex situations. For example, our theatre recently developed and produced Wesley Middleton's play Unsorted which has language that is both advanced and, in several instances, pure invention. Some parents in early readings wondered if it would be too hard for young people to understand, but a pediatrician in the work session stated that this sort of work was great for young people because deciphering new words in this sort of context could help to expand their verbal abilities. In performance, we found that children never had trouble understanding what was happening onstage, even when they did not fully understand the individual words being spoken."

Dwayne Hartford

"I have found that young audiences are willing and accepting of some language that they don't necessarily comprehend. In fact, I believe that young people are less likely to be pulled out of a play by an unknown word or foreign concept than adults are. Perhaps this is because young people are still in full-time learning mode. They are used to not understanding everything."

Celise Kalke

"Language should always serve the story. If the ideas are clear, the drama will be clear. Children understand Shakespeare very well, if the emotional content is appropriate and the acting is nuanced. Children also experience theatre in a second language much more easily than adults if the dramatic action is clear and the acting is filled. I think that worries about language 'levels' can impede the flow of thought. What is important for children is clarity of thought and utilization of their emotional accessibility. If these two things are present, language can be heightened and advanced. If thought and emotion are murky, then the language has to be very accessible because you have little else."

Jeffrey Revels

"The language level would depend on the story being told and the artistic director or artistic committee would know which demographics for which they are selecting shows. If we are talking about the use of profanity, then I advocate that we steer clear of that language. I understand that theatre is a mirror to society and that may be how people talk, but I think that we as artists can easily show that our points can be effectively made without resorting to profanity."

***

Just as playwrights may wonder if some language is "too advanced" for TYA scripts, they may also ask if their plays should include humor specifically for adults in the audience that young people may not understand (as often occurs in Disney films). Many TYA artists and professionals disagree with the notion that scripts should have 'separate' jokes and references for different ages, feeling that a script true to its characters that lets its humor arise organically and trusts its story as well as its audience, will ultimately have a wider, deeper, and more satisfying effect. Jennings argues emphatically against the use of segregated humor, arguing that "a script that uses puns, sophisticated jokes, or innuendo to amuse the grown-ups while going over the heads of the main audience is unacceptable in children's theater" (*TYA* 3).

TYA and "education"

Some playwrights may wonder if their plays must be "educational" in order to be produced or published. In a survey of 332 TYA professionals, K-12 educators, university faculty, and funding agencies regarding this topic, only 4% of respondents agreed with the statement: "All shows a TYA company presents should be primarily educational." A strong majority (76%) agreed that: "While the shows a TYA company presents need not always be overtly educational, companies should strive to make connections to education through study guides, post-show discussions, in-school workshops, or other activities." Finally, 20% agreed with the statement: "It is not necessary for TYA companies to produce educational programming, nor is it necessary to make connections to education through other tools" (Omasta n.d.).

Clearly, most respondents felt that TYA companies had a responsibility to make connections between the work they presented and educational purposes. However, most also felt that it was up to the producing company to make these pedagogical connections; it does not seem imperative, therefore, that all *plays* for young audiences be inherently didactic.

We asked our respondents if TYA plays needed to be educational, and while answers varied based on the needs of various theatres, most if not all agree it would be a mistake for playwrights to be overly concerned with this matter. In short, if a producing company likes a script but feels that it needs an educational tie-in in order to successfully market a production of the script, it is up to the theatre to educate the gatekeepers, or to the theatre's marketing team to identify and highlight this connection.

Do TYA plays need to be "Educational?"

Adam Burke

"I think that smart plays are educational but that smart playwrights don't set out to educate. If theatre is being used as a tool to educate then it should be called something different like 'school.' Plays should entertain, challenge and reflect, and examine the human condition in all its imperfections whether they are humorous or horrifying. That is why I don't personally produce plays whose purpose is to educate. If the primary purpose of a script is to teach or educate then we as parents and administrators will often overlook things like dramatic action, conflict, and character development and without those it is impossible for me to care."

Jeff Church

"Yes, to put it bluntly. At our theatre, yes. That said, we don't need them to teach a moral lesson. However, there must be a tie. Sometimes at the holidays, you can get by with a play that the teachers will come to as a 'field trip reward' for their students. In general, teachers tell us they need to justify it to the principal in order to come to us. That said, I'm not convinced that every teacher is teaching a lesson plan to their classes before or after coming to the play. Sometimes I feel they need for the play to look educational enough on paper."

Debbie Devine

"There is a ridiculous emphasis on education in TYA. Quality theatre is by its nature already educational. Theatre is 'what if …,' not a message, as the brilliant artist Andy Manley says."

Steve Fendrich

"No matter what show is given to children, the experience of watching a play is educational. Watching a play in itself is a learning experience. In this world of staring at television and computer screens, watching a play is often its own learning experience."

Mark Lutwak

"Theatre requires that its audience walk in the shoes of others. This is an inherently educational activity, one that requires us to exercise the most important social learning of all: we are all human. Call it the Golden Rule. For better or for worse, most theatres will tell you that it is name recognition, not educational value that sells tickets. Schools want to know that they can tie the work into the curriculum. It is up to the theatres to educate the gatekeepers (schools and parents) how any good play can be central to a child's life and education."

Judy Matetzschk-Campbell

"I think that all of our plays are educational by the very fact that all of our productions provide young people with a cultural experience. Do all of our plays have to have a direct tie to the curriculum? No. It might help with ticket sales, but I don't believe that is how to create meaningful theatre."

Writing for "sub-fields" of TYA

There may be an age group or particular branch of TYA that a playwright finds especially interesting. In order to explore practical approaches and concerns related to writing in some of these sub-fields, we looked to respondents who specialize in specific areas. This section is by no means an exhaustive exploration of every facet of the rather limitless field of TYA. It is, rather, a selection of some of the more unique markets, methods, and audiences that can from a practical standpoint, be approached in appreciably different ways. We explore TVY, theatre for teens, touring shows, puppet theatre, musical theatre, multi-authored works, and plays written for young people to perform.

What should playwrights consider when writing a play that is primarily intended for Very Young Audiences (0–5)?

Olivia Aston Bosworth

"Spend some time learning about the developmental growth of children under five years old. Consider length, vernacular, and points of participation. Every few months of these children's lives they develop new abilities, making them such a unique audience. Young parents are more and more aware of these milestones, so they are looking for opportunities to help their children grow."

Lauren Jost

"Let go of what makes 'good theatre' for older children and adults and think about the world from the perspective of a young child. They are captivated by unexpected magic, by

cause-and-effect and repetition, by striking visual images and rich sensory experience. Follow your own curiosity about a certain object or place or creature and don't worry too much about a traditional conflict and character development. Rather, explore a tangible problem that must be solved, or a place that must be explored. But don't forget about the adults in the audience – the show must be beautiful and engaging for adults as well!"

Barry Kornhauser

"Consulting with experts in the early-learning field can be quite helpful. They have taught us, for example, that very young children come in contact with reality less on a linguistic-discourse basis than on a bodily-sensory one. This suggests the use of multiple stage languages beyond the spoken word, eschewing dialogue in favor of physical and visual vocabularies, and a highly interactive, multisensory form of engagement with our audiences, transcending the traditional role of passive viewers/listeners. The very nature of very young children compels this."

Michelle Kozlak

"Any show written for very young audiences should really embrace the audience it is written for and focus on the clarity of the story or action. Be extremely creative. Be very honest. Offer a strong visual or sensory experience. Don't worry about traditional structures – TVY allows you to throw all those to the side. There is no right or wrong way to create TVY shows – that is the beauty of this genre. And last, but not least, don't underestimate the audience – they are very clever and intelligent."

Andy Manley

"I see a lot of work that is too complicated. That is not to say that it has to be simplistic but it has to be understandable for our young audience. There is no point presenting a world to very small children that they have no understanding of. Characters can be unknown, as can the world but a substantial amount in it has to strike a chord with them. I find it useful to write down what you know about each age. What things does a three-year-old like? What is their daily routine? What is a two-year-old's understanding of language? Can they jump? Run? Similarly if you don't know something it's worth writing the question down so you find out. This is a good foundation for making a show. This way you keep them in the room when you are making the work. I will often even sit where they will sit, at the height they will sit. Be them in the room, it helps. All these things help us to understand the world in which they live, and consequently make better work for them."

Mark Sutton

"The thing is to avoid symbolism, to dwell in the realm of a real moment, to be there with and for the very young human. It is a gift to share that dimension, to embrace wonder. So

slow down. Allow silences. You must try to see things as though for the first time. Listen closely to every tiny sound, such as the noise a piece of paper makes, or liquid being swallowed. Probably the most important thing is to allow oneself to play because this work is really a metaphysical journey in cause and effect. And truly a regression to one's own earliest sense of possibility. To do things over and over again to explore their nature, seeking the spark. When something tickles or surprises you, energy is released – and you know there's something there to capture and to share.

Our scripts start as outlines less than a page long. We have a notion of character and theme and a few basic plot turns. Then we have multiple play sessions in which we amass a number of objects and instruments we have imagined to be some part of the 'story' [...] we try things out, we discard things, we discover. We go shopping, we make things. The script gradually evolves between these rehearsals. Do not make the mistake of forcing 'interaction' with this audience. There is a delicate threshold of intense alertness in which a very small child's whole body is engaged in watching and listening. Another thing to strive to maintain – and this is difficult to accurately talk about, but – it's honesty. If we start to perform or push toward an emotion, we can very easily destroy an opportunity to authentically connect. Aim to do whatever is being done without artifice. Simply allow the young spectator to be present with you. It really means essentially removing the actor's mask."

What should playwrights consider when writing a play that is primarily intended for teen audiences?

Jonathan Dorf

"Understand who you're writing for. That means writing about subjects that interest teens, with plays that ask the kind of questions that they themselves are asking in their own lives. Do not write down to them, preach, or moralize at them. That annoys most of us, and teenagers in particular, because for many, it probably seems like that's all adults do. If they wanted a lecture, they'd go to one. In other words, bring your 'A' game as a playwright. Teens are young adults. They may not have all of our life experiences, but they can be every bit as sophisticated and discerning as adult audiences, generally with more honesty (and less filter).

I love working with teen actors, because they are, by and large, fearless. They are eager to grow and prove themselves. So challenge them and give them the moments to shine and prove themselves that they crave. They'll appreciate that far more than feeling like you're dumbing things down. Don't try to be overly cool or current, particularly when it comes to dialogue. Lingo changes, so it's better to create compelling characters and strong stories without trying to be quite too specifically 'of the moment.'"

Larissa Fasthorse

"When I wrote my first play for a multigenerational audience I was told: 'just write a play, we can take out the swear words if we need to later.' That's what I've always done with any

age. Write a good, compelling script that is honest to your characters. Once you've done your work, get some teens to read it for you. They will let you know what doesn't ring true as far as dialogue. I choose not to get too deep into specific slang, because by the time you get the play produced it will have changed. The teens give me a perspective on how things are coming across to their specific experience in culture and time."

Finegan Kruckemeyer

"All that one would consider when writing for any other demographic – I do feel that when a writer too pointedly considers a specific type of audience member (whether referencing age or anything else), they are in danger of undermining the creative exercise. They are curtailing where a narrative may go, because of how it may be perceived. And in truth, there will be myriad perceptions, offered up by myriad viewers, whether they are teenagers or adults or children. And so the notion of a generalized teenaged response is, for me, a problematic thing.

As such, I try to simply consider strong narrative journeys, and character arcs, and risk, and redemption, and hope and loss and whimsy and weight. I try to think about how to write the best possible play I can (it is never the outcome, but always the aim), and load it with enough permission and allegory and points of access that any audience member may interpret it as he or she sees fit."

Jonathan Rand

"My best advice would be to write something you would write for an adult audience but to challenge yourself to make a joke land or a moment resonate without having to drop an F-bomb or resort to nudity."

Pat Wilhelms

"Teen audiences want to relate, they want real-life dialogue. They like lots of emotion, very dramatic situations, and a good story! They want to see people like them in heightened situations."

What should playwrights consider when writing a play that is primarily intended for touring?

Rachel Briley

"I will describe some of the venues in which we perform as well as some of the limitations we face in our touring production. We perform in cafeterias, gymnasiums, etc. when we tour to schools. We seat the children on the floor (often in thrust, sometimes in the round) and play intimately in these spaces. The playing space is at times defined by a drop cloth as the floor, at times with a backdrop, at times with scenic elements that define the perimeter of the

space. The relationship between the actor and the audience is quite strong as the children are in such close proximity to the actors. We are required to bring everything to the school, and we travel in an eight-person bus with storage space that allows for minimal scenic/costume elements."

Mark Lutwak

"Touring varies from organization to organization; the missions, resources, and audiences are all different. If you are writing to an end, then partner with a producing organization. They can fill you in on their needs. My organization needs plays that are directed at three different age/developmental levels, are 45–70 minutes long; can be cast with three to seven actors from a company of young adults, can be loaded in and out in 45 minutes, and can be produced with no tech support beyond sound. Other touring groups have completely different criteria. They may tour to just one age group or tour one play to a wide range of ages, produce plays that are longer or shorter, have smaller or larger casts, have access to a different range of actors, require a show that can walk in and perform in five minutes. Others may load in overnight, and tour with lights, a 45-foot semi and six technicians."

Jeremiah Neal

"If you want to write a play specifically for touring keep the cast small! Think three to five actors maximum. This allows the most affordable tour for many professional companies. You also want to think about 45–50 minutes in length. This is optimal for school schedules."

John Newman

"A playwright creating a script specifically for touring should experience a touring show as an actor or stage manager. Hauling set pieces and costumes to dozens of performances gives a writer a clear sense of what is essential and what is unnecessary in telling a story in a less than ideal theatrical environment. Playwrights who have experienced a touring play as a performer or manager will rely more on the actor's ability to create the characters and less on the designer's ability to achieve the spectacle."

Tim Parati

"The budget and mode of transportation is key to this question. The bigger the budget, certainly the more you can provide. For us, we have to fit a whole show, basically, on one cart. They can then roll the cart holding the set of the show they will do that day into the playing space, unload, setup, do the show, strike, and load the cart up again without having to take countless trips to the van or trailer. Our players have three shows on three carts in the trailer and may do one show in the morning and a different show in the afternoon. Keeping the scene locations to a minimum helps. The more locations, the more scenery is needed. Special effects can also be tricky but usually can be pulled off in a 'theatrical' way."

Rex Stephensen

"Most professional touring shows that I have seen use three to four actors. Sometimes this is just not enough people to tell the story adequately. I have seen adaptations with three actors and the plot was so thinly told that I would not have understood the play if I did not already know the story. This approach has led to some very weak scripts."

What should playwrights consider when writing a play for puppet theatre or that incorporates puppetry?

Nancy Aldrich

"When writing for puppet theatre, there needs to be a reason to use puppets, as opposed to simply using live actors. Stories with animals, fantasy characters, any non-human character may best be played by puppets. Also, puppets can do things that humans can't: they can transform, defy gravity, and lose body parts."

Jon Ludwig

"First it is imperative to have seen a puppet production. In order to write for the puppet theatre it is critical that the playwright understands the basics of what puppetry can and cannot do. Puppets can be broken down into four general types: Shadow, Hand, Rod, and String. Each has their advantages and disadvantages. There are many examples to be found online but seeing a live production is best. Second, puppets are visual and physical. What they are doing is more important than what they are saying. Keep the dialogue to a minimum. Third, puppets bring the fantastical to the stage. They easily defy gravity, change scale, and embody the supernatural. However, if an actor can do it better, use an actor."

Paul Mesner

"Writing for puppets provides great opportunities and pitfalls. If the writer is very familiar with puppetry in all its forms then an idea of what is possible will help shape characters, plot, and staging. If the writer is not familiar one may not fully exploit the puppet to its full advantage. Understand the limitations of puppets and exploit them. Don't self-reference the fact that the puppets are puppets, this is just as annoying as an actor confiding to the audience that they are just an actor."

Mark Sutton

"Puppets are amazingly powerful. They offer a magical bypassing of your standard verisimilitude. We don't see the actor engaged in artifice. Instead, the animated object is fully the other, the authentic character. This simultaneously offers a tremendous freedom for the performer and an inexplicable, essentially magical fascination for the audience.

71

Puppets don't want to be talking or singing all the time. There should be fewer words in a puppet play. Simple, clear actions are best. Let them look about, breathe, think. A good bit of their lives onstage should be about simply reacting. I think the playwright creating action for puppet characters has more of an obligation to visualize gesture and shift of focus. Also, to consider whether or not the puppeteer will be seen and what this will say to an audience. If the playwright takes the time to prescribe all of this, the resulting performance can be astonishing."

What should playwrights consider when writing a play that is primarily intended for musical theatre?

Matt Buchanan

"If you expect or intend that your musical will be performed by young casts, as opposed (or even in addition) to professional adult performers, I believe you have a moral obligation to make sure that the music is appropriate for young voices. This means the proper vocal range, the proper level of technical difficulty, and, maybe most important, the implied singing style. It may be cute for a tiny tot to belt out a number like "Tomorrow" in the style of Ethel Merman, but she absolutely should not do so. It's just not healthy for her developing voice.

Here are some other thoughts about the songs in a musical, whether intended for child performers or simply for child audiences: Ever since Oklahoma, there has been an assumption that the songs in a musical should further the plot, rather than simply exist as diversions or changes of pace, as was the norm prior to that play's creation. It's not always followed, even in very good musicals, but it's a good rule of thumb and it's even more important when writing for children. Something needs to happen in every song.

Similarly, I try to avoid long slow songs or long sad songs. It would be insulting to assume kids can't handle a story with sad parts, and I do put sad songs in my work, but I keep them short. You really want to keep things moving. I actually aim for a point where I'm asking the child audience to stretch a little – to develop the focus and patience to slow down some – but not pushing it past the point where they lose interest. In terms of musical style, the sky's the limit, but I would caution you to avoid the temptation to be too 'contemporary.'"

Maggie-Kate Coleman

"Structure and function are everything in a successful musical, and musicals are not often structured like plays. There are a lot of rules (all waiting to be broken, of course, but know them first so you can break them with intent)! Read musical theatre libretti and see how the songs function dramatically. Learn how to song spot; learn which moments will make good song moments, and learn how music works dramaturgically. If you are going to write lyrics, study the masters and learn some basic song forms (e.g., AABA, Verse Chorus). Ask yourself, 'What is this song doing? How is it moving my story forward?' See, read, and listen to as many musicals as you can."

Jeremiah Neal

"Think about recording the music as both a cast recording and a 'karaoke' version with just the music. This can be costly and time consuming but is necessary to publish. Familiarize yourself with music lead sheets because the publisher will want to see those too."

Jonathan Price

"For any audience, the playwright should ask if there is a reason for music. In other words, does the story sing? Also, if the song does not advance the action, there should be something special given in exchange. If a song is simply dropped into a story, making the audience wait until the end of the song before they can find out what happens next, the song better be something special. In my own work, I try to have most songs advance the story. When I spot a book, I'll pick a whole section and replace it with song. This ensures that the story continues through the music. When my songs don't advance the action, I make sure there's something special onstage."

What are the things to consider when writing a multi-authored play?

Maggie-Kate Coleman

"It's important to have signed collaboration agreements in place when embarking on a project. If there are three collaborators, it is customary for each collaborator to own a third. It can be more complicated when there are two, for example, a bookwriter/lyricist and a composer, or a bookwriter and a composer/lyricist. I'm not a legal expert, but I believe the industry standard is still to think of it in thirds, though with many of my projects we have done a 50/50 split in the spirit of collaboration. It really depends on the project, but it is important to hash this out early on, not necessarily in terms of compensation, but in terms of clearly stating what each collaborator's role is and what they will bring to the project.

If you do not have a signed collaboration agreement in place stating that each collaborator owns their contribution to the project, I believe the law defaults to joint ownership, which can become really complicated if there is a dispute later on. Theatre writers (lyricists, librettists, and composers) have no union to protect us as craftspeople. We do not receive health care, nor are there minimum compensation terms that will increase as a result of collective bargaining. What we do have is the ownership of our work, and collaboration agreements are necessary to protect that ownership. Luckily there are many good resources for writers out there. I've found the Dramatists Guild to be a great resource, especially regarding legal matters. They offer sample agreements to members, and general guidelines for legal agreements.

On the non-legal side of collaboration, things are never clean-cut or easily separable. The lyrics and book I write would not exist without the composer, nor would their music exist without my words. Each inevitably informs the other, and it's crucial to maintain a balance of autonomy as an artist and flexibility as a collaborator. It's important to not be too precious about things, and always make sure that the entity in the room whose needs are primary is the piece itself. Musicals take a really long time to write, often five to ten years from inception to production (though the digital age is changing this a bit). Embarking on a collaboration of this kind isn't (or shouldn't be) a casual decision. You are linking yourself to your collaborator(s) possibly for many, many years to come. While your show is in its infancy, it's best to clearly articulate up front what the roles of each collaborator will be and what you expect from each other and the collaboration."

D.W. Gregory

"It's about getting clear about the work and why you think the piece is aimed at the audience you intend. Do they see it as something for very young people, for middle grades, for teens? Do they intend the young people as audience or performers or both? Do they understand the limitations of a TYA contract?"

Jeremiah Neal

"When there are several writers involved, it is important to have an agreement about rights going into the project. Don't wait to figure this out at the end; people will get upset. This arrangement might be different for each project; the most important thing is to keep the work moving forward. (Remember the publisher will get a large share too and other producers may think they have a stake. Keep the arrangement clean with fool proof contracts if necessary)."

Jonathan Price

"Every situation is different, but the usual split is 1/3 of monies made, and a credit order of 'Book by..., Lyrics by..., Music by...,' It can be anything, though, depending on what the team agrees to."

Writing for young actors

Playwrights should bear in mind that there are professional actors (both child and adult) and amateur actors (both child and adult). Age and expertise/training are not necessarily correlated. While in most cases a cast is primarily or exclusively either professional or amateur, a production could include a mix of performers at differing levels of ability and experience. The next set of responses deals with respondents' views regarding:

What should playwrights consider when writing for young amateurs?

Matt Buchanan

"One thing that works particularly poorly with young casts is a combination of young and adult central characters. When all of the important characters are adults, the audience fairly quickly forgets to worry about the fact that the actors are not. But an audience constantly presented with the contrast between a kid convincingly playing a kid and one trying to play an adult will inevitably wind up focusing on the less successful parts of the performance. This really only applies to central characters and it only applies when both the child and the adult characters are meant to be serious and naturalistic. This problem is much less pronounced if the cast covers a wide age range, with pre-teens playing the kids and teens playing the adults, but that limits the number of productions. Most school drama programs don't cover a range of more than about four years.

If your target cast is younger than dating-age, don't write a play whose primary dramatic question concerns romantic love. It's not that they won't understand it, it's just boring if you haven't experienced it. You also want to write characters that young people can play well. Characters that are far from their personal experience will be more difficult for them. It doesn't mean you can't write such characters, but it's not a good idea to put one at the center of the drama.

The most important challenge young performers have relates to time. Your play is going to be performed by kids with a million other things on their plates besides memorizing their lines and rehearsing. I try not to write plays in which a single character carries the lion's share of the weight. It's not about ability, it's about rehearsal time. You don't want any one kid to have too enormous a memorization task; ideally, you want to share the drama between several lead characters. If kids are going to have only two lines, you want them to really love those two lines. Over-the-top and comic achieves this much more readily than subtle can. I believe it is a great mistake, when writing dialogue you hope young people will want to perform many times, to try to reproduce the colloquialisms and mannerisms of contemporary teenagers. Teenagers hate to be condescended to, and while they'll appreciate a note-perfect rendering of the way they hear themselves, anything short of perfect will feel like parody to them and they'll resent it."

Jonathan Dorf

"It would be easy if everyone who performed our plays was a top-notch professional, but the reality is that if you're writing for young people, unless you only write for professional TYA actors, that's not going to be the case. You're going to have some amazing young actors, and some who are novices or are differently abled in various ways. I stumbled into a pretty successful solution for this largely by accident: when I was writing Dear Chuck I was told I'd need to accommodate over 30 actors. It's very hard to do that with a conventional play, so I wrote that particular play with a series of episodic scenes that cohered around a theme.

Later plays use a similar structure, with a mix of recurring characters and others who go in and out of the play, as well as choral/ensemble moments. Thus, directors can tailor their casting to their pool and offer challenging roles to certain actors, great moments to shine to others, and, to still others, opportunities to participate."

Anne Negri

"In writing plays for performance by youth I often take into account their age, theatre experience, and time/ability to memorize lines. Ideally I've had a chance to get to know the young people who will be performing and I can tailor the story to their needs. I also try to write equal sized parts. In this way, all of my students feel like they have their moment to shine and it keeps the amount they need to memorize to a minimum."

Jonathan Rand

"Many of my plays contain smaller roles or cameos, which can open the door for less seasoned young performers to cut their teeth on a more manageable acting experience. Shorter, more self-contained scenes can also help for the same reason, while also making rehearsals easier to schedule."

Dorothy Webb

"I personally don't advocate children under the age of ten being in an all child cast. I much prefer that they work in devising and creating their own scenes. I wouldn't advise anyone to set forth to write plays for specific age groups to perform. We have too many plays written for children to perform by well-intended folks who know little or nothing about play structure but want/need to create a play for 'all of the children' of whatever grade or group they are concerned with. My belief is that playwrights should write plays that excite them. When a playwright has accomplished that, he/she can decide if it is appropriate for child actors. Most children memorize fairly easily, but some roles can be beyond their ability to create emotionally or mentally."

Producers' needs

This section explores the resources various producers have available to them and how those resources can influence their needs (and therefore their selection of a particular script). These resources and needs vary immensely between producing companies. The responses below from respondents affiliated with some of these companies illustrate the variety of backgrounds and areas of specialty theatres offer. Some playwrights may therefore wish to anticipate producers' needs based on where they picture their work being produced (e.g., Youth Theatres, schools, churches, community theatres, professional TYA companies).

It should be noted, however, that while these playwrights may envision particular circumstances for their plays, there are no assurances the play will ever be produced under those circumstances. If a playwright is fortunate enough to have his play produced more than once, it will likely need to be flexible with regard to various factors. Playwrights seeking multiple productions may want to avoid including unnecessary limitations in their scripts that render them unproduceable in some contexts. The questions below explore potential considerations and limitations, but it is important to remember that these are *only* considerations. As many respondents express, playwrights ought not to allow themselves to be stymied or paralyzed by concerns beyond their control. Bob Moss adds, "Playwrights, it seems to me, should write about what concerns them, writing out of their own particular instincts, hurts, memories, and desires. Even *if* one is trying to write for a particular market. Writing 'to order' so to speak, seems to me to be a little deadly."

Is there a typical length that plays should run for particular age groups?

Nancy Aldrich

"For preschoolers: 25–30 minutes, elementary students: 40–50 minutes, middle school: 60–75 minutes would be my ideals."

Jonathan Dorf

"Plays targeted at certain markets tend to fall into certain lengths. For high school, contest one-acts that come in at 30–35 minutes maximum are most in demand. If a play runs 50–55 minutes and its only application is high school, it's not long enough to be a full evening, and it's too long for a competition, festival, or even a class period; it may be in theatrical no man's land."

Stephen Fredericks

"I do believe for pre-school an optimum time is in the area of 30 to 45 minutes. As a child grows, so too does their attention span, so that I believe that there is the opportunity to challenge with longer pieces as they go from elementary school to middle and finally high school. We are currently performing A Year with Frog and Toad which has a running time of 1 hour 15 minutes without intermission for grades K-3. I believe that time frame works well to 4th grade. Fifth through High School can go up to two hours without difficulty. We have done longer shows for family audiences, but with a fifteen minute intermission included mid-way."

Jenny Anne Koppera

"Currently at Spinning Dot, we are experimenting with ideal running times. We love to create work and perform for a truly family audience – from 1 to 100. Our longest productions currently run 45–70 minutes with no intermission. We also have newer productions in process within the main company and in our youth company that are approximately

20 minutes long that also seem to be fruitful for our audiences – especially for family audiences and for those school audiences under seven years of age."

Lisa Portes

"Our running times are dictated by the school schedules and are capped at 90 minutes. We do not run longer than 90 minutes because the kids have to get back to school. Generally we produce work that runs between 60 and 80 minutes regardless of age."

Rex Stephenson

"It seems to me that a determining factor in the running time of plays for young audiences is the venue. If we assume that the average roadshow finds children sitting on a tile floor in a cafetorium watching a performance, more than 55 minutes would seem to be as much pain as we would want to inflict on a small child's bottom. In addition, it's been my experience that often schools are notoriously slow loaders, and it may take them 15 or 20 minutes to get the school children seated for the performance. So if this is true, we are expecting a kindergartener to sit quietly for well over an hour. On the other hand, a lot of auditoriums are really not suited for children. The seats are geared for adults and in a 1500-seat auditorium with a balcony, the actors appear to some of the children about the same size as they do on a television screen. So in both these different venues, I tried as much as possible to keep my shows around 50 minutes."

***

To summarize: many touring companies prefer shows that run 60 minutes or fewer. TVY productions often run between 20 and 45 minutes. Plays for older children, adolescents, and families might run between 60 and 120+ minutes, though many professional theatres prefer shows running 90 minutes or fewer. Time constraints are often related to schools' scheduling needs. In 1998 Jennings contended:

The playing time for the majority of scripts for children is 60 to 75 minutes. A number of outstanding plays, however, last longer, some even with a planned intermission. Normally an intermission is unnecessary and undesirable due to the chaos that can ensue as an audience of 400 children chooses to go to the restroom. Re-establishing the story line and mood after extended scene shifts or an intermission can be difficult. A well-written and thoughtfully staged script should capture the attention of most of the audience throughout the performance without an intermission."

(TYA 3–4)

However, playwrights should not feel that they must limit their plays to 90 minutes or less. In fact, many longer plays are frequently produced, including, for example: *A Christmas Carol* by John Jakes; *Anne of Green Gables* by R. N. Sandberg; *Around the World in 80 Days* by Mark Brown, *Disney's Beauty and the Beast* by Menken, Ashman, Rice, and Woolverton; and *Mother Hicks* by Suzan Zeder.

What advice would you offer playwrights regarding venue-specific and/or particular technical requirements in their scripts?

Michael J. Bobbitt

"I try to make sure that the story holds its own without the use of technology. This will allow theatres that don't have the technical capabilities the potential for more successful revival. This allows for creative interpretation. I have seen subsequent productions of my plays and have been very surprised by new ideas that stem directly from what I wrote, but would have never thought of. Additionally, technology continues to change so fast. The technical element that you write into your play can possibly date the play. The same can be said for venue specific writing. We all want our plays to have a life beyond the original production. There is a potential for limiting the number of subsequent productions because of technology and venue specific scripts. I do often encourage playwrights to mention cool design, technology, and Venue Specific elements in stage directions, with a qualifier (e.g., 'in the original production, this character was created using projection')."

Matt Buchanan

"Most professional companies have access to fairly sophisticated lighting and sound systems, and while they may not be able to afford to build enormous sets, they at least have access to the kind of expertise necessary to deal with (or work around) multiple scenes and complex environments. But if you want your play for young performers to be produced a lot, you've got to write something that will work in a "cafetorium" or a "gymatorium," and that does not depend on complicated lighting effects, etc. You want to avoid anything that requires complicated scene changes that will intimidate the often untrained directors.

I approach this in two ways. I try not to write huge numbers of different locations, and I try not to write essential technical effects. But, being an artist and not a mercenary, I don't let such concerns prevent me from writing the play I want to write. So I also try to do some of the director's thinking for him/her. When I write multiple scenes I make clear in the stage directions that they can be done simply, and I explain how. The same goes for any kind of complicated effect. I'm always careful to use language like 'might' or 'could' when including this kind of 'director-proofing,' because I don't want to compromise the director's creativity, nor do I want to lose out on those producers who actually want to do a big, splashy production, but I try my best to make it clear that the play need not be prohibitively expensive or difficult in any technical sense."

Nikki Harmon

"Keep your tech requirements within reason and if they're unique requirements, always include in your script how to do them. Even simpler ones, like a snow cradle, might be easy for you, but the group may never have built one before, and you don't want your play rejected *because they don't know how to build it. If the design is complicated, find a less complicated alternative to include with the more complex version. Think budget."*

Mary Rose Lloyd

"Works for young audiences should be given the same consideration as any other theatre production. How will a particular venue support the artistic integrity of the work? Is the story best served by an intimate setting or a larger theatre? Creating work that tours to a myriad of venues provides an opportunity to play with flexibility of space."

Samantha Macher

"As a function of my theatre career, I have been asked to produce plays in some pretty dubious spaces, so before I even put pen to paper, I always try to imagine the "worst-case scenario" space and then resign myself to the fact that my play will only ever be produced there. Goodbye, Carnegie Hall, hello, small, un-air-conditioned classroom in southern California in August. I know this sounds bleak, but realistic visions of your work will help you get your shows up. I've produced plays in hallways, parks, and rooftops (as well as really nice theatrical venues), and the good news is that because I've had to figure out how to make theatre anywhere, I don't find it especially limiting to work in impossible parameters anymore.

To illustrate this point I'd like to use the cafetorium as a case study of sorts. It's basically the devil's multipurpose architecture and almost every school has one. Because this probably isn't what you had in mind when you were creating your whimsical world of fantasy, this might be a disappointing reality unless you think about the space like a producer. Think of it through that lens and suddenly you'll see its perks as well. For one, you do have a lot of flexible space to work in, and a built-in audience of children and parents forced to attend your show. So instead of requiring your 20-person musical about thunderstorms to be produced in a proscenium with strobe lights and a fog machine, perhaps you might consider allowing the option of students breaking the fourth wall to move freely through that mandatory audience (improving the acoustics), or indicating a rainstorm by shaking some tin (reducing the budget).

In my experience as well, more often than not, if you allow for everything except the text and very important stage directions *to be interpretive, the resulting piece will be better than you imagined. Trust me when I tell you that there are few more creative theatre artists than children and the mentors who create a world for them to act in (on a $200 budget). I highly suggest that you allow your collaborators the space to do their job. Don't micromanage them from afar with elusive technical requirements; instead, give them flexibility to tell your wonderful story. If you give the directors and producers the freedom to work within their limitations, your play will be doable!"*

Is there an ideal cast size for TYA and Youth Theatre plays? Are there preferred gender breakdowns?

Matt Buchanan

"There are specific things that producers of plays with young casts look for, some of which are different from or in some cases the opposite of what producers of professional productions with adults look for. Most obvious of all is cast size and demographics. In a professional production, every cast member costs money, so small-cast plays are more likely to be produced. But most directors of plays with kids want to give opportunities to as many kids as possible, so they look for plays with large casts. They're also typically dealing with a wide range of ability levels, so they'll want to find a play that offers several meaty roles along with plenty of less challenging parts. Finally, in most school drama programs girls significantly outnumber boys, so you'll want to keep that in mind. Plays in which female or gender-neutral roles predominate are better bets."

Nikki Harmon

"There are groups that tour (usually with a cast of five) and ones that want larger casts. If you write a play for ten actors, and you can find way for five roles to be doubled, you'll have two bites of the apple. Most of the theatres/schools/groups have more girls and women than boys and men, so the more roles you can write that are gender flexible, the better."

Rex Stephensen

"The first non-touring show I wrote was an adaptation of Robert Louis Stevenson's Treasure Island. Basically there are two problems in dramatizing this script. The first is that there are numerous other adaptations. Secondly, the show requires almost no women. This is a problem for almost all high schools, and it was always my problem at the Blue Ridge Dinner Theatre. The solution I came to was having Robert Louis Stevenson take the idea of his story to his stepson Lloyd's teacher and ask if they would play through the action and create a play that he might craft into a book. Therefore, the cast, which can be as big as 25 characters, can be done with only two males. I think the success of the show owes a great deal to this flexibility in casting."

Very first draft complete: What next?

After having taken into account all relevant ethical and practical considerations, a playwright may compose his first draft and then be unsure of what to do next. We therefore asked respondents what they suggest regarding the next stages of script development. Though their methods vary, each stresses the importance of collaboration and hearing the script aloud.

What should playwrights looking for opportunities do once they have completed their first drafts?

Larissa FastHorse

"I encourage hearing the script out loud right away. Yes, apply to workshops and such, but first get your friends together, cook them a meal and have them read your script. It's the easiest way to determine what is coming off the page and what is in your head. If you have some kids handy, invite them! They are your audience. Watch them, ask them. Listen."

Dwayne Hartford

"Network. Go to gatherings for the TYA community where new work is being promoted. Meet people, and promote yourself. I have found that the TYA world is populated by some truly wonderful and friendly people. After completing a first draft find a group of people to read it aloud so that you can hear it. (This is where you'll see what's in your head but not yet on the page.) Your critique group is fine for this purpose. Later, you may want to round up some high school or college actors to read the script. When you think you are ready, seek out an organization to give the script a developmental workshop. Be prepared to listen to feedback, not argue. Be available to do rewrites every night! Consider having a few questions for the audience to answer in writing after each performance. But remember, it's your script, your baby, and you are the one who must make the final decisions. Then submit the script to one of the many possible contests or somewhere where you can have a full production mounted."

Amy Jensen

"Ask for feedback from people whose critical and creative thinking you like and trust. Hearing from them what stands out and is tantalizing about your play as well as what may be confusing can help you pinpoint what to develop, clarify, and cut. If you're looking for general feedback or if you have a specific question, ask a writer; they are often willing to read and respond to a fellow writer's play. For a more in-depth response or if you want someone to give you feedback over several drafts, hire a dramaturg. If you sense that you need to hear your work in order to track the dramatic or theatrical progression of your characters, the story, the conflict, and so forth, put on a play reading. Invite actors to read your play, even if it's just in your living room.

Designers ask great questions about both dramaturgical and practical issues. If possible, try to ask people who know you and/or your work. Try to be open to feedback, but asking for feedback doesn't require you to make the changes people suggest, especially if the feedback feels too proscriptive and/or off-target. If possible, pay people what seems fair to them and to you; it establishes a level of professionalism and respect on both sides. Research your opportunities.

From the many play development competitions, retreats, festivals, or new play reading programs, find those whose missions, aesthetics, and stated or implied phase of development (early, middle, late, or essentially finished) is a good match for you and your play. Particularly seek out local organizations; they may have a mandate to work with local writers, which can increase your odds and help you build your local network of people whose critical and creative thinking you like and trust."

Kristen Leahey

"I would recommend entering contests, going to graduate school, looking at the theatres in your community, and starting to work with them and see if eventually they are interested in working with you. Build local relationships that build to national relationships that build to international relationships."

Anne Negri

"Share. When I am working on a play, particularly in its early stages, I feel some fear and reticence to share a draft with others. I am usually afraid that something is poorly written or characters are broad and stereotypical, etc. However, if someone asks to read a draft of your play, that is a gift. Say yes! Even if you don't end up agreeing with their feedback, you have to keep sharing in order for your play to have a chance beyond your notebook or computer."

David Saar

"Find a partner theatre that believes in your belief. Again, that sounds simplistic, but Childsplay's best work over the years has come out of long-time collaborations with writers. Out of ongoing relationships and trust will come the richest material. Writing is such hard work, and that can be eased with a collaborative partner. Theatre is about artists working together to create a vision that is better than any one of them could have done on their own. Allow other kindred spirits into your creative process – it is my belief that it will help you become a better and deeper artist."

Suzan Zeder

"Here's what I do when I've completed a first draft. I arrange a reading with friends, loved ones, etc. in a very informal, no pressure environment. Because my usual writing retreat has been in a very small town in rural Colorado this most often means that I will not have professional actors – often not even actors. Some of the folks who have read my first drafts have never even seen a play, much less read one. This is a humbling and sometimes terrifying experience as it will probably be the worst and best reading the script will ever have. Best because there is absolutely no pressure for it to succeed, best also because the group invariably

loves *the script (or maybe it's the green chili stew I serve afterwards) but they always say "It is perfect, don't change a* thing." *But I know I will probably change everything before I am done. What is most helpful to me is that this will be a reading for real people, not a theatre or university crowd. The responses and perceptions I will get are from everyday folks, not those who filter through their own expectations and opinions. They will reflect back to me what they have seen heard and felt, and that is worth all of the critical discourse in the world.*

A first draft is too raw, too new for any kind of critical discourse. It would be like giving a grade to a baby. But you can share a baby with loving friends and see how it smiles, hear how it laughs, watch how it teeters on baby feet trying to walk – that's what a first reading is like. I will also hear absolutely everything that is wrong with the script and not be embarrassed by it. I will know there is plenty of time to change things, but, *when something works, when a moment rings true, it will shine like pure gold, unadulterated by an excellent 'performance' or an informed opinion! I do not recommend this 'trial by fire' approach for the faint of heart. It sometimes takes an experienced writer to know how to separate what is in the room from what is actually on the page. Too good a first reading will cover the very flaws you are trying to discover, too bad a reading can cause you to lose confidence. So it is a delicate balance.*

Once you have a few more drafts under your belt I recommend another reading, this time you need *good actors and a rehearsal period. You need to hear more than a cold reading will tell you. Luckily in our field there are some excellent new play development programs. These can be highly competitive and not everyone gets in, but they are excellent places to develop new work. Another great place is at a theatre where you respect the work they do. It may be a TYA Theatre, a Community Theatre, a College or University Theatre Department. All are great places to 'play' with your work. But do not wait for these opportunities to come to you. You must be proactive and seek them yourself. You will be building the collaborative relationships that can last a lifetime!"*

∗∗∗

In this chapter we explored practical considerations to keep in mind before, during, and after initially generating a new TYA script. Our next chapter touches upon some of the specific opportunities and challenges of writing adaptations, both from a creative and legal standpoint. From there, we will move on to the next steps of the journey of a new script.

Chapter 5

Adaptations

If a playwright feels drawn to adapt literature or other source material to the stage, there are aesthetic and business-related questions she might first ask herself, such as: Is the source material she wants available for adaptation? Is it in public domain or does she need to procure rights? If the latter, how does she go about doing so? If it is written by a living author, how should she plan to go about working with that author and/or the author's publisher? How will she go about adapting from an artistic perspective? And perhaps most importantly, *why* does she want to adapt a particular source material? Answering these questions and pursuing the necessary steps requires her to have a willingness to do a great deal of footwork and soul searching.

This book does not provide legal advice, but rather shares stories and explores how playwrights might avoid potential pitfalls. We also recommend readers consult Appendices A and B, which provide additional texts and resources to help navigate this often complex and potentially difficult terrain.

Business concerns

Most theatre professionals familiar with adapting tell playwrights that their foremost logistical concern is to make sure they have permission to do so. If the work is not in public domain, playwrights should obtain the rights to use the source material before beginning the artistic process. Dana Singer warns: "If you write an adaptation before obtaining permission, you are taking a huge risk that all the work will have been done in vain and will have to be discarded if permission is ultimately denied" (66). Singer discusses the steps of this process in detail, including how to go about learning "whether the underlying work is still under copyright protection" (63), "whether the rights to adapt the underlying work as a play or a musical are available" (64), and finally, best practices for obtaining permission (66–106). If a playwright is ultimately granted rights, she should ensure that this permission is in writing. Creating and implementing a written contract with the author or their representative *prior to adaptation* takes time and research, but may ultimately save a playwright from potential grief and frustration. These contracts often allow for one-time use, but may also include options for a future extension of this if all parties are willing. See Appendices A and B for additional texts and resources that may offer further help with obtaining model contracts, finding answers to other business-related questions, as well as navigating complex negotiations and relationships.

Many playwrights have stories of heartbreak relating to having spent their time, talent, and money on writing adaptations that never saw the light of day, or that enjoyed success but then had permission pulled for one reason or another. It therefore is advisable that playwrights do their homework. Another issue relates to resources allocated versus gain, both monetary and artistic. As David Morgan explains:

> As playwrights we struggle to gain access to source materials and when we do manage to get the rights, the royalty percentages on adaptations are so low that you almost end up paying for the right to adapt a book. Very few publishers will grant exclusive rights, so you can write a terrific script but nobody else can perform it.

Therefore, to proceed with adapting, playwrights need stronger reasons than profitability as well as an understanding of the risk that their work may not last beyond a single production. Below, we and our respondents share additional experiences adapting work.

What types of experiences have you had working with authors, agents, and representatives on issues such as obtaining rights to adapt a work, securing script approvals from authors, etc.?

Nicole B. Adkins

"I have written several adaptations, two that were not in the public domain. In both cases I contacted the author personally (via email and phone) to inquire about initial permissions; these were granted. Both authors were a joy to work with from the start of the process throughout subsequent development, productions, and beyond. Being new to the business side of adapting I did not know to implement a written contract prior to writing the plays. Though there were contracts in place between myself and the theatres and the book authors and the theatres, I did not realize that it was incumbent on me to also create a separate contract with the book authors (nor were they aware of such a need). I was very lucky that in both situations the authors and the theatres involved felt positively about the scripts and were invested in their longevity, as well as being extremely generous and easy to work with. From what I have heard, this is not always the case."

Sandy Asher

"Years ago, Amie Brockway commissioned an adaptation of Walter Brooks's Freddie the Detective. *The rights were secured, the script was written, the premiere was wonderful – and then the agent announced that there was a snafu in the rights she'd sold earlier to not one but two movie companies and they'd be tied up in the courts for quite some time. Our stage rights were eventually restored – but only for five years, not long enough to interest a publisher. My 'revenge' was to adapt one of my own books,* Too Many Frogs. *I granted*

myself the right to do so, and promised never to take back my word! It turned out to be a healing and joyful experience."

Dwayne Hartford

"I was very fortunate, in that working on The Miraculous Journey of Edward Tulane *with Kate DiCamillo's people was incredibly easy and pleasant. I had to get her approval of a working draft of the play. I emailed the script to her agent, and got back an approval within a week. That was a very happy day for me."*

Y York

"I have great respect for novelists and my source material. However, my allegiance is to play structure and to the scale that is the stage. My adaptations veer greatly from their originals. When I'm talking to a novelist, I share my previous adaptations; I tell my process; I invite the author into the development of the script. I have received great and horrible notes from authors. For the production, I have the deciding vote, but often the author has the right to prohibit future productions if s/he feels the play is unworthy of its source material. You have to be comfortable with this arrangement. The story is not yours. I had a great experience by asking a novelist to read the draft aloud, after which he came more fully onboard. Always have the rights before you start. Always be clear about 'the deal.' Read and understand and make sure you agree to everything in the contract before you sign on."

Market domination

Recent studies suggest that TYA companies are increasingly likely to produce adaptations of popular children's/YA literature, though original plays are still produced as well (Hanson). Hanson notes, "scripts that were adapted, in whole or in part, from literary sources, comprise about half of all TYA plays produced today – more than twice as many as a generation earlier" (196). He argues that the reasons behind this are largely economic, relating to marketing toward the ticket-purchasing demographic of guardians and other gatekeepers, who are more likely to expose the young people in their care to stories with which they are familiar.

The artist who aspires to write original work may feel discouraged by looking at the seasons at theatres offering TYA and family audience work; she may feel that in order to ever have a chance at having her work produced she must begin to devote her time to writing adaptations. However, Jeff Church notes: "Don't [adapt] for the money because there's nothing there. Do it because you're passionate about telling that story, and try to tell it in a theatrical and original way" (as quoted in van Kerckhove 36). Similarly, when we put the question to respondents, though many are realistic about the great prevalence of adaptations in TYA, most do not suggest writing with profitability in mind.

Is writing adaptations more lucrative (in terms of income, productions, etc.) than writing original plays?

Sandy Asher

"If you're very good at what you do, make the right connections, and get really lucky, you're likely to make more money writing adaptations than original plays or even historical pieces, even though the last two may be curriculum-related. I was once part of a focus group for a professional theatre. The group was limited to season ticket holders. The #1 reason given for getting off the sofa and going to the theatre – by far – was: 'I saw the play before and I liked it.' The vast majority of theatregoers want to be entertained in a comfortable way. No surprises. They choose plays for their children and grandchildren in the same way. Teachers are no different, except that they need to find a curriculum tie-in to justify the expense of taking their children to the theatre. Thoughtful, daring, original plays carry a risk factor and that's reflected in ticket sales. (One director jokingly told me: 'You can write whatever you want, as long as you call it Cinderella').

I've done a lot of adapting over the years and those plays tend to be produced more often than others. But those adaptations have not been done with the bottom line in mind. I'm sure there are people who are able to work that way quite successfully, but I'm not one of them. I have to fall in love. I have to want to spend months – maybe years – exploring a story, living with it and inside of it, discovering the best way to bring it to the stage. I have to be so excited about it I feel I must share it with the world."

Adam Burke

"Our company is more likely to produce an adaptation because of our partnership with the Charlotte Mecklenburg Library. Economically though, it makes sense in the same way that it makes sense to do a revival. Hopefully the book has already generated a following of some sort that the theatre can capitalize on. It is probably more important for a writer to know their audience. If the writer is submitting a play to a company it behooves them to research the company and understand what the aesthetic is. Finally, the most successful playwrights I've known have been very diverse in their writing."

Nikki Harmon

"If you're not going to write an original piece (which is very hard to get produced because almost all schools insist on established source material), you can get around that with a Cinderella tale set in a village in Uganda that deals with a step mother who insists that going to school is for boys, or on the outskirts of Mumbai that deals with forced marriages, or in the Australian Outback that deals with prejudice."

Steven Ivey

"Most sponsors want a show that their audience has heard of or read in book form. It's easier to 'sell' a popular name title than an obscure one, so I encourage the playwright to talk to *their local library about books that are 'hot' and try and find ways to transform that book into play form."*

Mark Lutwak

"If you are a playwright who wants to adapt literature, then by all means write it. It is important that such plays be as dramatic, honest, and well-written as any other material."

David Saar

"I am probably a Pollyanna, but I truly believe that playwrights should focus their energies on whatever story they are passionate about, whether that be an adaptation, an original work, or a piece that springs from personal experience. I think that it is only there where they will discover their authentic voice. If you begin writing with a primary eye to perceived marketplace desires, I think that chances are good that you will create more McPlays."

Michelle Wright

"Adaptations [of popular books] are easier to sell to audiences and schools, and many of them make great pieces of theatre."

Artistic approach

If a playwright plans to adapt source material (to which she has the rights), she may wonder how to approach this from an artistic standpoint. First we examine some practical challenges, including: audience expectations, questions of essence (how faithful does a playwright want or need to be to the source material?), how to bring a fresh slant to a story that has already been adapted many times before, and length of the source material versus length of the play.

Regarding audience expectations, Deborah Wicks La Puma notes: "It's really hard for [audiences] not to have expectations, particularly if they love the story and that's why they've come. Our take on the story might be very different than the way they see it" (as quoted in van Kerckhove 33). This can also be connected to questions of essence – whether a play captures what an audience (and the playwright) first found compelling about the source material.

Playwrights vary greatly in their approaches to maintaining the original story; every source calls for a different approach. One playwright may feel that a particular work calls for an exact as possible translation, while another may view that same work simply as a launching point. For example, there are countless adaptations of *Cinderella*. One may be a literal translation of particular versions (e.g., by the Grimm Brothers) while another could use the same original text to launch into a fantastical journey set in outer space; others may use different source material of the same story.

York describes her process adapting *The Witch of Blackbird Pond*, and her search for the essence of the text: "I was so excited because I'd made this play where there had been no play, out of this incredibly vast, sprawling story that takes place over a year" (as quoted in Engelman 26) However, when she went to the theatre to read the play, there was much disappointment. She left upset, but was inspired by her husband who suggested "a page-to-stage thing." She realized she had taken the "danger" out of the play and strove to work it back in. York notes:

> I don't even think I changed the structure; I think scene for scene they're probably identical, but the content of every single one of those scenes changed. And every element, either from the book or elements that I had introduced, became dangerous, instead of elements of joy and discovery and welcomingness – which is what I had turned the story into.
>
> (as quoted in Engelman 26)

As to bringing a fresh perspective to a known tale, Deborah Wicks La Puma argues for the potential usefulness of adapting as "a way for kids to experience a story or character they love in a whole new way, to see it from a different perspective. It helps them see the world at lots of different angles" (as cited in van Kerckhove 32). The prevalence of fairy tales, folk tales, and other widely adapted stories can bring in centuries of precedents and audience expectations. Furthermore, examining these stories closely may raise questions for the playwright regarding the inherent ideology. A playwright will want to ask herself how the embedded messages relate to modern audiences, and – if that playwright decides that certain messages are no longer resonant or possibly even damaging, whether she can reframe the question in order to make it a worthwhile exploration for a modern audience. In 1974, Lifton argued against adapting fairy tales without great care and artistic attention.

> Not that I am against fairy tales, for their truths have been distilled through the centuries and have the power to reveal us to ourselves. Rather, I am impatient with those who manipulate and distort them for a few easy laughs. One cannot help longing for original artists to breathe new vision into these classics, to release their powers and let them reflect the absurdity, the terror, and the wonder of the age we live in.
>
> (12)

This is still a widespread topic of conversation today among TYA professionals.

There is the question of length, which again can connect to audience expectations. To look at extremes: how does one go about adapting a book with no words, for example? Or a 300-page novel? Again, the answer depends on so many factors, including (but not limited to): the source material itself, the adapting playwright's vision and voice, as well as many of the practical considerations noted in the previous chapter (for example, is it a commission project? If so, what are the playwright's stated tasks and limitations?). Jeff Church describes his experience adapting an epic tale:

When I did *A Tale of Two Cities* years ago, I was taking a book with so many subplots and had to decide what was important for the story that I wanted to tell. I cut out some pretty major characters. And so there was some [feedback] from people [asking] "How could you cut him?" Well, not easily. But I'm writing a TYA piece, so it has to stay at the hour-and-a-half range.

(as quoted in van Kerckhove 33)

Ultimately, each adaptor must balance factors including satisfying audiences who love the original, serving the needs of potential producers, preserving the essence of the original story, serving their own artistic vision and ideologies, and how to best translate the story into the language of the stage. To get a sense of the variety and complexity of artistic approaches and challenges inherent in this work, we asked several respondents to describe their own experiences and techniques.

From an artistic perspective, how can one approach the process of adapting?

Sandy Asher

"*In the original book* Too Many Frogs, *Rabbit reads several stories to Froggie, an eager listener, but we don't know what those stories are. For the play version, I shared those stories with the audience by having Rabbit's bookshelf turn into a puppet theatre while he reads to Froggie. Because Froggie is an intruder into Rabbit's quiet life, I chose three 'intruder' stories:* Goldilocks *is about a destructive intruder, which is how Rabbit sees Froggie at first. The* Elves and the Shoemaker *is about helpful intruders. Could this possibly be the case with Froggie? And* The Ugly Duckling *is about an unappreciated intruder who turns out to be something quite wonderful – a swan. And, indeed, Froggie also turns out to be something quite wonderful – a friend. The stories were chosen for several reasons: to lengthen the adaptation of a book that takes about five minutes or so to read, to bring theatricality to the simple act of reading through puppetry, to present variations on the theme of 'intruders,' and to offer classic, available stories that families could then share at home as Rabbit shares them with Froggie.*"

Matt Buchanan

"*What works for one adaptation won't necessarily work for another. The first thing I do when approaching an adaptation is to explore in great depth why I want to adapt that particular work. What is it about the work that speaks to me, and what is it about the work that I think speaks to others. (This is different than asking why I think the work will make a good play. Whether it does or does not depend entirely on how well I do my job.)*

Two practical examples: One of my most successful (at least in terms of sales) adaptations is a version of Little Women. *Having begun the project by re-reading the novel several times, I reached the conclusion that the most appealing thing about it was the voice of the* author. Louisa May Alcott draws the reader into the warmth of the family and their day-to-day trials and triumphs through her familiar and warm literary voice. I believe that's what folks really remember about the book, and what they love about it. So I decided that my approach must retain Alcott's voice as much as possible. But I didn't want to stick a narrator in the corner of the stage (ugh!) so I finally hit on a sort of 'Story Theatre' structure, in which all of the characters alternately narrated and entered into the scenes. In this way I was able to retain large chunks of Alcott's language closely enough to retain the personality of the author. This structure had the additional benefit of making it easier to cram two huge volumes into a single play of manageable length, because it allowed me to fill in the gaps where I had necessarily skipped over events in the story. To further respond to the familial warmth that I felt was the main appeal of the novel, I structured my play so that it centered on a single fireplace that, with minor prop changes, served as both the Marsh family hearth and the hearths of several other homes in the story. As written, this hearth is the only fully realized scenery in the play. The hearth functions as the central metaphor of the play.

By contrast, my Shakespeare adaptation, Two Dudes from Daytona, retains not a single line of Shakespeare's language. My goal here was partly educational and partly because it's one of my favorite Shakespeare plots. My approach was to retain the structure of the play almost perfectly intact, even though all of the characters and their specific situations would be contemporized. Heading to the city to make one's fortune at court became heading to New York to break into Broadway. The bandits in the no-man's-land outside the city became a goofy 'gang' of kids. A lot of the characters were gender-reversed (mostly to create more female roles). But the plot structure was left intact. At the same time, language is one of the reasons I love Shakespeare, and I wanted to retain some of that poetic force. I rejected the idea of writing in verse, which I assumed young casts wouldn't enjoy and young audiences wouldn't get. Instead, I set the play in highly stylized versions of surfer-culture Daytona Beach and slick hipster Broadway. This allowed me to play with language in a poetic way without making it obvious or off-putting. What unites these two very different approaches is the fact that I let the source material and the reason I liked it dictate the approach I took."

Melissa Cooper

"I love creating new plays from classic texts. Those texts have long ago proved they can stand the test of time. Anyone can get hold of them. You can read them, talk about them, wrestle with them, play with them, or use them as a shotgun propelling you into current issues. The original texts are in no danger of disappearing or losing their value, no matter what you do. To my mind, the greatest danger the classics face is being put on a pedestal and approached with kid gloves.

I always read the original text many, many times, and then do mountains of research all around it. I never know exactly what I'm going to write about ahead of time, so the reading and researching is my way of stumbling around in the world of the play, getting lost, and *then found, and then, probably, lost again. Eventually something emerges that starts to lead me on. Usually I start to hear voices, dialogue, and if I track those voices attentively and nonjudgmentally, like a tracker following footprints in the woods, I'll find the people I want to write about and their story starts to reveal itself. In some plays, like* Antigone Now, *I've stuck fairly closely to the structure of the original text. In other cases, the original text has served as inspiration for a very different play, as with* Little Medea *and* Red Badge Variations."

Dennis Foon

"*For young audiences, I've adapted* The Hunchback Of Notre Dame, *and two of Volker Ludwig's German plays,* Bedtimes And Bullies *and* Trummi Kaput. *The Hugo novel was daunting because it's a vast novel with a huge cast and ripping story. My job was to figure out what I loved about the book and to try to find a way to stage it. I conceived it for a small cast playing multiple roles on a bare stage. My goal was to remain true to the book. Volker's plays have a very specific cabaret-like style, and with that comes a very un-North American sensibility. The challenge with those plays was finding a way to maintain the incredible humor, energy, and drama and yet make them accessible to North American young audiences.*

In recent years, I've adapted many novels for film, and many of the same questions apply: What is it about this book that I love? Can I adapt it and stay true to the heart of the novel? Is the medium I am adapting this piece for the appropriate one? If, for example, it's the stage: what can theatre techniques do to illuminate this piece visually and emotionally? These questions become my spine in making decisions about what stays and what goes. This job of selection is a tricky one, but if you stick close to the emotional core – and proceed with a lot of respect for the material – you have a decent chance of creating an adaptation that will satisfy fans of the book – the author – and yourself."

José Cruz González

"*I once did a community-based project involving mariachis. I interviewed many of them and even went on a gig. These musicians were by day working class folks, but on weekends they would transform into mariachis. The* traje *(suit) they wore and music they played would transport their audiences. I then read* Don Quixote *and found a way to tell their story through that great novel. We performed with mariachis in Boyle Heights on a December evening. It was magical.*"

Dwayne Hartford

"*The biggest challenge with* The Miraculous Journey of Edward Tulane *was that DiCamillo's story is a beautiful narrative of the physical and emotional journey of a china toy rabbit that neither speaks nor moves. How do you write a play in which the protagonist is an inanimate object? The answer turned out to be beautifully theatrical and, I'm happy to say, quite effective. An actor who moved throughout the space, while never manipulating the rabbit, voiced the thoughts of the toy."*

John Newman

"In developing an adaptation in a workshop setting, I have found that it is beneficial in the early phases to work with actors who have *read the book and in later phases with actors who* have not *read the book. When the adaptation is in the conceptual phase, it is helpful for the playwright to hear what the other actors bring into the story, since audiences familiar with the original might also bring those ideas and interpretations to the performance experience. When the adaptation is nearing production, it is helpful for a playwright to focus on what connections are and are not being made in the script, independent of how those elements are connected in the source material."*

***

In this chapter we touched upon some of the important artistic and logistical considerations of adapting source material to the stage. We turn next to New Play Development.

Chapter 6

New Play Development

New play development (NPD) can mean a lot of different things. Some NPD festivals, competitions, and other events provide formal opportunities for playwrights to workshop scripts-in-progress with a team of theatre professionals (often a professional director, dramaturg, and actors). Playwrights fortunate enough to participate in such NPD events experience a forum where everyone involved is primarily dedicated to making their script stronger, as opposed to focusing a production for public performance.

Often, plays do not have the opportunity to be workshopped until they have been selected for production by a theatre company. Theatres vary widely in how they approach the production of a new play. Some may employ a process resembling the NPD workshops above. Other lucky playwrights may have the opportunity to collaborate with a director who is committed not only to creating a strong stage production in the short-term but also to helping the playwright shape his work in ways that will increase its longevity. Still other theatres involve playwrights to lesser extents, perhaps only asking periodic questions. In some cases, a theatre will not involve the playwright at all in the rehearsal process after deciding to produce it and paying the appropriate royalties. Unless a contract specifies otherwise, theatres are not obligated to include playwrights in their production process. Many will however, as it can be mutually advantageous when working on a new script.

The end of chapter four introduced a variety of options for a playwright looking to move to the next step after having completed his first draft. This chapter is dedicated primarily to working in formal NPD workshops and processes, such as the biennial New Visions/New Voices (held at the Kennedy Center) or Write Now (formerly the Bonderman symposium) (held at either Childsplay or the Indiana Repertory Company). A more extensive list of these opportunities is included in Appendix C. Some of these opportunities are documented in detail; Newman's dissertation "Spotlight on Process" analyzes all aspects of the Bonderman, for example. Suzan Zeder notes that such festivals are "excellent places and programs helmed by wise and compassionate leaders who are totally dedicating to developing and promoting new and exciting work for this field."

The main topics covered in this chapter are similarities and differences in the processes of developing new plays for young people and other audiences, the benefits of incorporating youth into the NPD process, and the roles of various NPD collaborators, as well as how to most effectively work with them. As indicated above, for the most part, this chapter approaches the subject as if a playwright were participating in a formal NPD opportunity (e.g., a week-long workshop) rather than working with the creative team on the premier of a new play. Some of the information will be applicable in either situation, but a major difference is that in most cases, theatres will place a much greater emphasis on creating a strong overall production for their paying audiences when rehearsing for a premier performance, while a NPD workshop will be more focused on enhancing a scripts' overall longevity. A playwright working on his first production should be sure to have a clear understanding with the producing company about his relationship with and involvement with the production.

New play development in TYA in comparison to other forms of theatre

The idea that plays can benefit from extensive workshops and other preparation prior to their first production did not originate in TYA. Readings and workshops are common in all forms of theatre; most Broadway productions are produced as staged readings and similar venues (often several times) before they make it to the stage. Many of our respondents have worked in both TYA and theatre for other audiences, and we sought their insights into how NPD processes were similar or different for these types of plays. There is no consensus on this question; some argue that the processes are clearly different, others that they are not, and still others' views fall somewhere in between. This plurality of views is important to keep in mind when developing new work for any audience: there are no "right" answers; professionals with rather disparate views succeed despite (and perhaps because of) their varying approaches and beliefs. Ultimately, every script requires a unique process.

Is there a difference between the processes of developing new plays for TYA versus plays for general audiences?

Janet Allen

"I think the ground has leveled a lot between development processes for work for adults and young audiences in the past 10–15 years; historically, the difference was that there was a prevailing sense that young audiences work didn't need development, perhaps because it was shorter in format or largely adapted from literature, but that myth seems to have been dispelled by various new play labs devoted to developing work for kids. All new work needs development in some manner or other, in that playwrights need time and resources to test and refine their work.

That being said, not every work needs the same development tools, and now our systems are fairly reliant on playwrights knowing what their work needs and holding out for those needs or finding them. I have sometimes worried that TYA plays were rushed to publication prematurely, but I think that's less prevalent now. I think work needs smart dramaturgy, whether that dramaturgy is done by playwrights themselves, a smart friend or colleague, a director, or an actual titled dramaturg. But nothing should be developed to death either!"

Adam Burke

"Generally it isn't. The biggest difference I've seen is the inclusion of children in the creative process early on. So the creative team might do a staged reading or a workshop of the material for a group of age appropriate audiences and solicit feedback. I don't often hear about playwrights writing for adults seeking out an appropriate audience to include in the early stages of creation. I suppose that is because the playwright for adults assumes they know best whereas the playwright for children has questions because they are not a child."

José Casas

"From my experiences, developing plays for youth differs from developing plays for adult audiences because of the audiences trying to be reached. Obviously, dramaturgy plays an important role for both and due diligence in regards to any type of research is essential. However, in theatre for youth, plays deal with a variety of different age groups and the fact is that brains are still developing. It was once thought that the brain stops developing at the age of 18, but recent studies have suggested it is closer to 25 years of age.

TYA playwrights must understand their 'target' audiences in depth in order to write to youth rather than down to them; a result I have seen time and time again. I feel the idea of creating a dialogue with audiences becomes more imperative with youth audiences who, many times, react more honestly to the theatre they are witnessing than adults and part of that is because of their life experiences which I believe also need to be taken into consideration. For me, this adds a layer of complexity to the development of youth playwriting that adult playwriting doesn't necessarily have to deal with."

Amy Jensen

"In general the process is similar, but TYA's creators are only very rarely in the same demographic as their target audience. Although we were once children, we don't respond as they do. So some development processes, therefore, actively incorporate young audiences. To develop story or character ideas with young audiences requires working with young audiences at a very early stage of the creative process, so it is less likely to be used in a formal play development process. Organizations like Write Now invite young audiences to watch and respond to a staged reading at the beginning and end of the development process. Several organizations invite young audiences to the final reading or production, which acts as a kind of litmus test."

David Kilpatrick

"My instinct is to initially say 'no' – that each playwright wants to write the best play possible for their audience, whether they are adults or young audiences. No matter the audience, it still comes down to the story, the main characters' journeys, and whether or not you have a clear beginning, middle, and end. But as I reflect on this question a bit further, I do think

part of the development process needs to differ, because so much work for young audiences needs that input from young people during its development. This means thinking through ways to workshop the piece in front of school audiences or bringing young people into your rehearsal room – something that I don't believe you're as concerned about when developing so-called 'adult' plays."

Kim Peter Kovac

"If it does, I don't think it should. A play is a play; good writing and dramaturgy are good writing and dramaturgy."

Kristen Leahey

"TYA inherently thinks about the audience, which all theatre disciplines should. In 'adult theatre' we're seeing a progressive change in audience engagement, where artistic staffs are conversing with the audience about their responses to the work. It's something we've been comfortably doing in TYA for a long time, such as what Charlotte Chorpenning did in the 1930s with her reception studies and what we see with NPD symposia today. I think interrogating the audience and thinking about them in terms of artistic development is something we do well in TYA that I'd like to see across the board but in a way that offers playwrights support and allows them to differ these processes if they are not helpful to theirs."

Dorothy Webb

"Any NPD should serve the playwright and the play in whatever ways will help that specific playwright, regardless of the intended age of the audience. One difference might be that NPD of plays for young audiences will profit from adding age appropriate respondents to help playwrights test whether or not what they are doing is working."

Suzan Zeder

"Not so much anymore. When I first started writing the development process took place entirely within the rehearsal process. You were lucky if you had a 'reading' before the first day of rehearsal. I remember one TYA director tell me that his developmental lab was his season. I also remember when the word 'dramaturg' was a totally unfamiliar term in TYA and much less a presence in the rehearsal room or in a developmental process. Now there are college and university classes in writing for and about young people; most of the major professional TYA companies take years to 'develop' a script through readings, and sometimes in residencies and partnerships with colleges and universities.

There is both an upside and a downside to this developmental 'progress'. Some scripts get developed, but never produced, particularly if they are original scripts not based on familiar titles or adapted from books and movies with built-in marketing opportunities. While there were fewer 'developmental' opportunities for playwrights when I started writing there was far more original, risky, innovative work actually produced by major theatres. I have built my career writing mostly original stories with a few adaptations thrown in, but today I doubt anyone would take a chance on fully producing a script called Step on a Crack *today from an unknown writer, not based on a Newberry award-winning book or a familiar classic or fairy tale."*

Previewing work with young audiences

One of the most commonly cited difference in NPD for TYA was the inclusion of young people at some point in the development process. Many playwrights have commented that hearing from people the age of their intended audiences is invaluable to their plays. Sean Bliznik and colleagues interviewed several finalist playwrights, directors, and dramaturgs at the 2009 Bonderman Symposium. The symposium provided playwrights with the opportunity to hear from young respondents. Richard Perez, who directed a staged reading at the symposium, "said he found the youth invaluable to the process. Many of the larger changes to the script came in direct response to comments the students made after experiencing the first reading. Perez said the feedback and comments helped bring the stories of the youth characters to the forefront of the piece" (Bliznik et al. 10). To see how universal this feeling was among respondents, we asked:

Is it important to preview new works before age-appropriate audiences?

Janet Allen

"I think it's key. How a room full of grown-ups reacts to a play meant for children is only one very small indicator and not a very good one. We started including youth audiences as the primary respondent/collaborators at Bonderman/Write Now over 15 years ago and never regretted it. Organizations that collect young people – schools, after school programs, faith organizations, community centers, camp settings – are generally hungry to be asked to participate in something new and different. Doesn't mean the logistics are easy, but [previewing plays before young people is] invaluable. Sadly, most kids don't get to see many plays, and are unfamiliar with how they are made, but bringing them into the conversation in groups helps ease that unfamiliarity and create lively interplay."

Maggie-Kate Coleman

"I find myself often discussing my own work (not work targeted at youth audiences) with my students and young friends because they're smart and they're interested. After years of doing this, it has become a litmus test of sorts for whether I really know what I'm writing about. By having to describe my story to a ten-year-old, I am forced to tell my story simply, clearly, and directly. Which is what I should be doing anyway, not just because I'm talking to a ten-year-old!

If I can't do that, then I know it's back to the drawing board. A few years ago, I was discussing a musical with an eight-year-old (one I'd been writing for years and thought I really had asked and answered every question that could be asked). After I gave him the rundown, he responded, 'Cool,' and then after a moment, 'Why?' 'Why what?' I responded. 'Why are you writing it?' I was stumped. I didn't have a simple answer. I am grateful for my experiences with young artists and young audiences. The most valuable thing I have taken away from these experiences is that my job as a writer first and foremost is to focus on youth audiences as audiences *rather than* youth, *and to trust and respect their intelligence, focus, insight, and ability to process complex ideas and themes as I would* any *audience, regardless of age."*

Kristen Leahey

"Personally (and others would disagree) I find when doing a new play that integrating the audience into the development process is essential. Working with groups (schools, drama, or English teachers, or any classroom that's really passionate about the arts) can be great. Sometimes you want to work with a group that has no exposure to theatre, other times you want a group that has a lot of experience with theatre. It depends on the show."

Amy Jensen

"Directly including a young audience in previewing new work can be useful in observing rather than predicting what is and is not working for the audience. Adults seek to represent the best interests of young audiences, but adults may underestimate or misjudge what is and is not going to work for young audiences. I once observed a performance with a school audience for a play in development by Carte Blanche. The play used multiple metaphors and images in addressing time, lifespans, and death. Although the students were attentive throughout the performance, afterward their teacher insisted that they could not have understood it. The company listened but didn't agree. Instead, they focused on identifying where the students were restless and revised those moments."

Jon Ludwig

"We have just now tried this out over a long range development process. We have worked with Georgia State University, which has an early education department. Workshopping the new work with pre-K through 3ʳᵈ graders a year in advance has given us incredible insight into how kids think. It radically changed the way we developed new works."

Paul Mesner

"We often preview the play we are creating for an audience. We try to have the creative team there so they understand firsthand any challenges the play gives to audience attention and comprehension. We partner with several underserved preschools and grade schools who regularly come to our other shows; they are often happy to come and be our preview audience."

Beth Murray

"*There is no better teacher than the young audience. And there is an art to fostering feedback (not fishing for compliments) in multiple modes and contexts. Frequently, we are so immersed in our projects that we narrow in on what the kids can tell us, based on our criteria (aka our worry areas) within our play that we are sure is almost perfect. But the feedback, if we really tend to it, screams otherwise, perhaps inconveniently otherwise. Having a person separate from the process (e.g., not the director or the playwright) facilitate the feedback process is key. Those gifted in gathering responses and mining kids' minds through art and play and writing and process drama, not just through large-group talk back, will help frame the young people's criteria for making meaning of the play. Their criteria are almost always richer than the adults' limited version.*"

Of course, not all feedback is useful, as Moses Goldberg noted as early as 1974:

You are seeking a conversation, a dialogue. Nothing is gained from an adult's convergent questioning of a child, or from an embarrassed silence. It is more difficult, many people believe, to engage a child in real conversation. It takes sincere interest in his point of view, and some care in phrasing open-ended questions.

(*Children's* 129)

To determine how playwrights might avoid "embarrassed silence" in favor of dialogue, we asked respondents:

What strategies are effective for getting useful responses from young people?

Nancy Aldrich

"*We invite some of our donor families to preview new work before it is performed in the theatre. While they consider it a special benefit of being a donor, they may not be aware how closely I am watching their reactions and attention levels. I have gotten great feedback from these events, from parents as well, most often about subtle language changes that I may not be aware of. An example is from our production of* The Ugliest Duckling, *in which the duckling is actually a platypus. I changed the Mother Duck's line from '[…] he's special,' to '[…] he's unique,' because a parent pointed out that 'special' has acquired a negative connotation because of the word's association with disability.*"

Amy Jensen

"*First of all, getting a group of young people involved usually entails finding and developing an alliance with a partner organization, a school, an after-school organization, or a youth group. Speak early on with leaders and teachers to explain how you envision this working and what role they will play. Discuss with them what they hope the students will get out of the experience. Because this is additional work for them, try to make it as easy as possible for them to participate. Make sure to communicate early on about the logistics of meeting each other, especially if it includes travel. In talk-back sessions after a play, I've observed that it helps to briefly relate that the playwright is continuing to write and rewrite the play, and that young people can help the playwright by sharing their thoughts and feelings about it. It's useful to mention that there are not right or wrong answers. Open-ended questions like 'what moments or images stood out to you?' can help start a talk-back. Some teachers might be willing to lead or facilitate post-play experiences, such as asking young people to draw or write a response. Teen audiences may be more hesitant to respond in front of you. You might learn more from what a leader or teacher tells you was shared on the way back from the play or perhaps in the days following the play, so keep in touch with them."*

Beth Murray

"Gathering kids to respond to a play requires that you are really clear about what you are offering. There are always eager groups of kids at schools, after-school programs, libraries, camps, day-care centers, etc. They are eager for a rich arts experience, especially if it's free! When you begin connecting with groups, remember this is a relationship you are building, so collaborate clearly and well within the group's parameters. They are getting a 'sneak peek.' They are 'helping you revise.' They are responding to a 'work in progress.' The leaders need to know: how many kids, what age, what space, what length of time, what preparation is needed, what the accompanying teachers need to do, why this is beneficial for the students.

It is usually easiest for you to go to them, but a field trip is possible with more notice and planning. Remember that schools will want to have as many kids as possible involved, for fairness. Hold fast to your maximum. It's hard to get good feedback from 350 kids at once. However, 350 kids could see a show, then you could deploy actors to individual classrooms for a 20-minute follow-up session with hands-on activities and discussion. Or you could perform for three groups of about 100–125. Or you could request a group of 25 for an hour.

Schools have strict policies about videotaping kids, so clear your methods with the office. Plan to have something other than video as your primary form of documentation. Having kids write and/or draw creates rich data. Use kids' time and energy effectively and efficiently. Think about what you want to hear from them before experiencing the play, and what you want to hear after. Think about the ideas you want to hear from every individual child, and those you want to hear/see kids building on each-others' responses. Plan accordingly."

Suzan Zeder

"I am increasingly excited by the possibilities of interaction with young people, not just in previewing new works but in the genesis of the new work itself. My newest play Aviatrix *is*

about women and girls who fly, literally and metaphorically. It has been commissioned by Imagination Stage in Bethesda, MD with an ongoing relationship with an innovative arts-based elementary school, The Lucy School in Maryland. When Dr Victoria Brown, the school's founder and director heard about the play she went to her teachers and they committed to a yearlong, curriculum-wide exploration of 'flight' with all grades Pre-K-5. I did two residencies at the school while I was writing the earliest drafts of the play, chatted with the kids, looked at their artwork, and recorded their voices. I have used direct quotes from some of the kids in the dialogue of the play, and in the recent reading of the play at the Kennedy Center's New Vision/New Voices we used their real voices in a sound collage at the beginning and ending of the piece.

This isn't a devised piece, but the kids have become a kind of living laboratory for me. The same group has heard two different readings of two different drafts: one at the theatre, one at the Kennedy Center. Their response and input is invaluable. To get truly genuine responses from a group of thoughtful and informed young people is pure gold. But to do this we have to radically re-envision how we ask questions, engage young people in discussion, and help them respond to the play from inside *the developmental process rather than standing outside as a traditional audience. In this way they become, if not collaborators, co-conspirators, in the developmental process."*

Qualities of effective NPD collaborators

In addition to helping strengthen a play, NPD festivals and workshops provide playwrights great opportunities to network with those in the TYA field, build relationships, and familiarize people with their style of collaboration. During a workshop, a playwright will likely interact with a wide variety of individuals who may or may not be working directly on his play (including management/administrative staff, designers, technicians, actors, respondents, etc.). For the most part, these individuals are involved in the program to serve the playwright's play. This does not mean, however, that they are there to serve *him*. While his work may be the 'center of attention' for the process, it is important to remember that each individual brings unique expertise to the process. The theatre world is small; TYA world is even smaller. You never know who will one day recommend you for a particular opportunity (or choose not to). Anyone with whom you come into contact may have some eventual influence over whether you ever work with a team of collaborators again.

Seattle Children's Theatre Artistic Director Linda Hartzell once noted: "I think the best thing is to not work with high maintenance people, you know, but rather mature, generous people who make the process fun and meaningful" (as cited in Engelman 27). This echoes a sentiment we heard in off-the-record responses from several respondents: in order to be an effective collaborator, "don't be a jerk." For more formal responses, we asked two artistic directors (of a TYA company and general-audiences theatre), a lyricist, and a dramaturg.

What qualities do you look for in playwrights with whom you might collaborate?

Janet Allen

"I'm looking for shared sensibilities about what theatre is and what it's meant to do for/with a community. I'm looking for an easy verbal communicator; I'm looking for someone that understands that while the work is important and precious, it is a thing unto itself; it isn't a person. I'm looking for a listener as well as a writer. I'm looking for someone with a fair amount of balance and perspective, and an ability to understand what production elements can and cannot bring to a play."

Maggie-Kate Coleman

"The quality of work is only one important factor when looking for a potential collaborator. While it is important that some of their previous work resonates with me in some way, it is often more important for us to be on the same page in terms of process. Do we or can we define collaboration in the same way? What is the timeline? What is your work ethic? How flexible are you willing to be? Can you take critique? Are you willing and able to give helpful critique and feedback? Do we get excited by the same things? Are you willing to duke it out over the important stuff without getting personal? Will you put the needs of the show above your ego? Are you willing to contribute ideas, or do you expect me to be the sole idea generator? Are you going to be precious about your work and respond to feedback defensively?

I often see advertisements from playwrights or composers looking for a collaborator to 'turn my [play, song cycle, etc.] into a musical.' This is usually a big red flag for me because it tends to indicate either a naivety of the writing and collaborative process and/or that they may consider their contribution to the final product complete. I look for collaborators who respect my role and contribution to the piece, but who are really willing to be equal partners in the creation of a new work. Above all, I look for collaborators who are interested in writing the same piece I am interested in writing."

Amy Jensen

"I prefer to work with playwrights at a point where they still want to revise their plays. I look for playwrights who are interested in open conversations so that we can both better understand each other's point of view and feel comfortable asking questions and making suggestions. Mutual respect is important to me, as is trust, particularly trusting that I will not rewrite or force a play to become something it is not. That trust is sometimes only won over time; near the end of a production an initially reluctant writer told me how much he appreciated that I was helping help him write his best possible play."

Janet Stanford

"I look for huge talent in a writer, whether new or experienced. Some of the playwrights we regularly work with are highly accomplished. Their 'voices' are already strong and clear. When

we do a development week with a writer of this caliber, it is usually more about defining a stylistic convention for the show and addressing the technical challenges it presents because the characters and dramatic arc are already there. With other writers, we get very involved in questioning any problems we see with the story, the paths of the various characters, the placement of songs, the choice of conventions, and any other element that strains credibility or feels less than satisfying. Sometimes, a playwright will go through five or six drafts for us.

It is always best when we as dramaturgs can pose questions or define choices for a playwright and then allow him or her to go away and solve these problems in their own creative and unique way. Our goal is always to remain sensitive to the playwright's experience and perspective from which the play derives but also to provide the sounding board that helps translate the play from inside the writer's head to the public arena where it must be accessible and connect with a large and diverse audience."

Working effectively with collaborators

Once one has chosen collaborators (or had them assigned), playwrights need to understand how to effectively work with the various theatre artists on their creative and production teams. One important thing to determine as soon as possible is what protocols are in place for communication with various parties, what you can expect from each team member, and what they are likely to expect from you.

In most cases, a playwright's direct interaction will be primarily with the director and (if available) dramaturg. In general (though there are exceptions) his communication with actors, designers/technicians, and other team members will be filtered through the director and/or stage manager (if present). There may be cases where the playwright is invited to collaborate directly with these individuals, but he should be certain that this protocol is appropriate (unless it has explicitly been mentioned, it probably is not). Communicating directly with designers or actors without consulting the director can cause confusion and could unintentionally harm the play and/or production. This does not mean a playwright should never acknowledge or talk to these important team members, but rather he should avoid giving them any sort of notes or direction; this is generally the director's job, and the playwright should work with the director if he has ideas or concerns regarding acting or technical elements. Y York recalls that at one time:

I'd write a play and I thought my job was to go to rehearsal and explain to everybody what they needed to do in order to make my play work. What I have learned is that this process is so much better when I write a play and I go into the room with these other people and I am quiet. I can see more clearly what is there for people to get, and when it isn't there for them to get it; I can see how to not blame them. Instead, blame the play because maybe – even though it's in my mind – maybe it's not on the page yet. That is an amazing thing that you get to discover when you have a development process.

(as quoted in Engelman 24–25)

There may be times an actor approaches a playwright directly and asks for his feedback. In these cases it is generally best for the playwright to thank the actor for her work but refer her to the director for feedback on their performance. Typically, the communication dynamic is made clear to all team members from the beginning of the process. If it isn't, the playwright should talk to the director, producer, or stage manager to see how they want to function and communicate it to the rest of the team.

How can playwrights most effectively collaborate with creative and production teams in the new play development process?

Janet Allen

"I think all theatre artists yearn for trusted colleagues with whom they can or have developed a shared sense of values and vocabulary. It simply deepens the work, and wastes less time. While as a producer, I can't always import a whole team to support a playwright, I always want a generative artist to have a colleague or two working with them that they know and feel safe with. So, if a playwright has a dramaturg with whom they work, or a director, I may very well want some of those folks on the team. I'd say that if it's a NPD lab, I sometimes feel the opposite – that's there's value in hearing a new viewpoint, particularly in a commission situation, where collaborators have been working a long time on something and still don't deem it finished."

Laurie Brooks

"In NPD, listen to what people have to say and then decide what resonates for you. Know how to avoid being reactive to criticism. Learn how to write down ideas and think them through without rushing to judgment. Then charge in fearlessly and try new ideas. Save those old drafts so nothing will be lost. Knowing that nothing will be lost encourages bold experimentation. It is great to hear what all interested parties have to say, but it is more important to remain true to your original intent. If you follow all the advice that is thrown at you, the work becomes written by committee rather than created by a playwright with a single vision and goal. Find a few smart people that you trust and make them your first (and best) readers. As a playwright, it took me a while to figure all that out. In more than 20 years of playwriting, I have found that the best dramaturgs for me are the fine directors I've worked with."

David Kilpatrick

"Theatre is already a small world, so when we start talking about TYA, we're talking about an even smaller world. So, relationships are incredibly important in a career. The next gig, promotion, project, etc. might very well be for that person you met at a conference or through another connection. First impressions are important, but even more is following up on something you may have discussed in your conversation."

Kim Peter Kovac

"Be a collaborator, yet don't let yourself be walked over. Keep a sense of humor. Don't get self-righteous. Focus on the project at hand, not on hustling some future relationship or job with that person. Learn from everyone. Thank people who help you."

Anne Negri

"A relationship with NPD collaborators takes communication. It may be that collaborators are not in the town where you live, so communication via email or phone is vital. Theatres are busy places and they are often producing another show or shows while your play is in development. Development can often be a long process, so you have to be patient, yet present. Follow up on communication in a timely manner, but don't assume that you and your play are the theatre's sole priority. If something is time-sensitive, like a deadline or a workshop, making a phone call may prove more satisfying than email exchanges.

Flexibility is a key component of a NPD opportunity. This is often the most difficult element of the relationship to balance because it is so delicate. As a playwright you must be flexible in terms of trusting others to embody and translate your story onto the stage. You have to trust that your collaborators understand and believe in your play and that they will creatively bring it to life using all of the performance and design resources at their disposal. Their vision may not match the vision you have in your brain. You must decide when a choice enhances, improves, or clarifies your play and when a choice is ultimately wrong. If a choice is not true to your story or characters, you should not give up and accept it. You need to pick and choose your issues wisely. If everything becomes a battle, then the relationships cannot be sustained."

Dorothy Webb

"Networking is vital so burn no bridges. Some collaborators may be too busy to pursue any further relationship, so always ask first if you are unsure about whether or not the person is interested in continuing contact. If they are then maintaining contact with those collaborators who have been the most helpful (not necessarily those most laudatory) can be helpful. Be respectful of their time."

Partnerships with higher education institutions

Some potential collaborators might be faculty in college/university theatre programs who may see value in developing a playwright's work at their institutions. This can lead to mutually beneficial relationships in which the playwright has his play workshopped while the university's students get to experience the new play development process and work with outside professionals. Laurie Brooks suggests that "colleges and universities are ideal places to develop new work. They have available actors, technical support, directors, and dramaturgs. These venues are not dependent on ticket sales and so are more able to take risks with new plays." For example, Adkins and Omasta first began collaborating when Adkins had the opportunity to develop a new play at Utah State University, which went on to be performed elsewhere and placed in a national playwriting competition. The experience proved so beneficial to all parties that they have gone on to develop two more plays through this process. Please note, this method requires not just the support of the initial faculty member, but also university administrators who generally decide if funding will be allocated to such projects.

The role of the dramaturg

While dramaturgs have been present in the theatre world for centuries, their appearance in TYA has been a relatively recent addition. While dramaturgs can serve many functions, in the NPD context they usually work closely with playwrights as sounding boards and consultants on script-related matters to help the playwright most successfully realize his vision.

Several playwrights from the 2009 Bonderman Symposium commented on the valuable input of the dramaturgs with whom they worked. Melissa Cooper noted that her dramaturg, Judy Matetzschk-Campbell, "gave me honest responses to two separate drafts, and I knew from her intelligence, theatre savvy, and humor that we'd be able to work well together" (as cited in Bliznik et al. 11). Matetzschk-Campbell noted: "As a playwright who has also worked extensively as a dramaturg, I believe that one of the most helpful things a dramaturg can do is to raise questions for the writer" (Bliznik et al. 11).

A dramaturg's job is not, however, to write the play for a playwright, or even to serve as a definitive voice. Ultimately, they can provide valuable insights, and in most cases playwrights would be quite wise to consider their input, but ultimately as Laurie Brooks has observed: "No one knows your play better than you. Trust that you'll recognize the advice from others that will be helpful. Then stay true to your authentic voice." Sandy Asher similarly notes:

> When I get a suggestion that interests me or comes from someone whose expertise I respect, I try it on. I take time to let the new way of doing things play out in my head. I may even sit down and revise the scene as suggested. But not always. And I don't always go with the revised scene even after I've written it. I may go in a different direction, or I may even go back to the original.
>
> (as quoted in Matetzschk-Campbell and Newman 159)

Both Brooks's and Asher's comments do not apply exclusively to dramaturgs, but to anyone who might give feedback on a script-in-progress. They both note the importance of staying true to one's work but also listening carefully to collaborators, and because of their role, dramaturgs are often positioned to give more feedback than anyone else in the NPD process.

To gain their own perspective on their role and how to best collaborate, we asked two dramaturgs:

What is the role of a dramaturg in the new play development process and how can a playwright most effectively work with one?

Amy Jensen

"*Although my role and degree of engagement changes with each play, I primarily give constructive feedback. I become very familiar with the script, studying how the playwright has used story, dialogue, character, and action. I seek to understand the structure of the piece, how it builds upon or breaks down upon itself, and, as frequently happens in new plays, where it has repetitions. I seek to read generously. I often do research, and if it seems pertinent or useful for the writer or creative team, I will share it. As early as possible, have a one-on-one conversation with the dramaturg that will help her or him understand the script's genesis and trajectory. Share what specifically led to writing this play. While your impulse may have changed, it speaks to the heart of the piece and the dramaturg can better understand your goals/vision and work toward them. Be frank about how finished the play feels to you and what you are most interested in revising or developing.*

If you, rather than a company, initiated working with the dramaturg, ask her or him about creating a contract. Establishing a contract is an opportunity to come to clear, shared expectations about what the dramaturg will do and how she/he will be compensated and recognized. The Employment Guidelines by the Literary Managers and Dramaturgs of the Americas (www.lmda.org) are a good resource. During the play development process, continue to be in regular contact."

Kristen Leahey

"*There's a tendency to assume that the dramaturg is the expert on the subject of the play immediately when they are assigned it. It is important for writers to know that dramaturgs often aren't selected for their expert knowledge on the specific topic, and often know less than the writer on the subject. Instead, they are often selected for their ability to ask good questions, for having intellectual curiosity, for being collaborators who are very invested in people and their art, and knowing how to access the experts. Dramaturgs need to be able to build relationships and anticipate things. They are organized and flexible and ok not being the top of the theatrical hierarchy, unless invited. Another important thing for writers to know is that they should provide as much information as they can. If you have things you like or don't like these are good things to tell the dramaturg; ask for what you want and don't assume that people just inherently know your individual needs.*"

Collaborators from outside the field

Finally, a playwright may be very familiar with the literature and practices typical to TYA or may be a newcomer. Either way, a playwright may find himself collaborating with individuals who have little or no familiarity with TYA and could harbor misconceptions about the field or its work. We therefore asked three veteran TYA playwrights:

Is there anything to consider when collaborating with individuals who are new to the field of TYA and may harbor certain problematic pre/mis-conceptions?

Sandy Asher

"I would suggest the collaborators comb the AATE Directory of Award-winning Plays for scripts similar in style or intention to whatever they're developing and then read extensively in the field. Reading back issues of TYA Today *and* Incite/Insight *might also prove useful. If possible, attend TYA festivals and conferences and see performances by professional TYA companies, Youth Theatre groups, university theatre groups with strong TYA credentials, and so on. The work of admired companies might also be sampled via websites and YouTube. The point of all this would be to demonstrate to the newcomers that the field has changed a lot since the adapted-folk-and-fairy tales-only days. See what the best are doing and then proceed accordingly! Finally, I'd suggest the playwright bring in a trusted and experienced colleague to act as dramaturg, either on site or long distance, to provide insight, information, and support. Workshopping the piece at other theatres with more experienced colleagues, even if with informal table readings, might also help."*

José Casas

"Working with collaborators who have no experience in TYA can be extremely difficult. I have been there and done that. Right off the bat, communication is the most important thing that must be established. If collaborators cannot effectively articulate their thoughts and ideas, a production is doomed to fail. The person with experience in working with youth must also take on the role of educating, to a certain degree, the people who do not have experience. They must try to get the other party to understand, not only the theatrical project they are working on, they must try to give the other party an insight into the field. Too many times, people in our field feel compelled to justify or legitimize our field when we should not have to. TYA practitioners/artists should create an environment that deviates from this mindset. In the end, both parties need to 'be open' to each other's thoughts and work toward creating a unified vision of what the production should be."

D.W. Gregory

"If you are collaborating with directors or designers new to TYA find out why they are doing the play. If they have no experience – what are they aiming for? Do you think

you're on the same page? Is there a conflict of vision for the project? If so, it may mean trouble."

***

In summary, playwrights who are able to participate in formal NPD experiences have the opportunity to receive extensive feedback on their work from a variety of professionals that will hopefully promote the longevity of their written script. If they are particularly fortunate, their work will be seen by age-appropriate audiences who they can (at minimum) observe to see their responses. They may even be able to have more extensive discussions with the young people in order to better understand their reactions to the piece as written.

NPD festivals and symposia also provide excellent opportunities for networking and building relationships. Serving as an effective collaborator will not only benefit a play but also the playwright's standing in the field as others learn who he is, what his work is like, and if he is the type of artist with whom they would like to partner in the future. In addition to the general principles of being professional and kind, it is important to observe the specific protocols in place at a particular workshop.

Once a playwright has had the opportunity to write and develop a script, he will likely be ready to pursue having his work produced and eventually published. The next chapter discusses these processes in detail.

Chapter 7

Production and Publication

The previous chapters have discussed ethical and practical considerations when writing original plays and adaptations, as well as how a script might effectively be developed through an NPD workshop. While new works might benefit greatly from additional readings, workshops, and feedback, eventually most playwrights will want to see their work fully produced by a theatre company and/or published.

This chapter discusses ways to pursue production and publication opportunities, in that order. Many new writers may aspire to have their work published as soon as possible, in hopes that it will then be more accessible to readers and potential producers. While it is possible that some plays may follow this route, in most cases publishers will only consider work that has already been produced (perhaps multiple times). As Pam Sterling notes:

> Finding the right venues for development, workshopping and/or production are more useful than trying to figure out what publisher you want to approach. Starting with the publisher is like putting the cart before the horse. First write a good play and see what kind of audience it seems suited for. While publishers are interested in art, the bottom line for most of them is whether the play will sell.

In many ways, this is advantageous to the playwright. As long as a script is unpublished, she can continue to revise it, and each performance will inform her understanding of how live audiences respond to her work onstage. Revising a play (even extensively) after a full production is not unusual and can make the work stronger. Conversely, publishers will rarely allow playwrights to revisit their scripts to make changes once they are published.

Given the traditional route of writing to development to production to publication, this chapter will continue in that sequence. We first discuss how playwrights can pursue opportunities to have their work produced, including exploring what artistic directors might look for in the plays they include in their season, as well as a brief section on self-production. We then turn to a discussion of if and when it is best to publish a script, how to find an appropriate publisher for a given script, and what publishers look for when deciding if they will accept a manuscript.

Getting produced

There are numerous ways in which playwrights might see their unpublished work produced, but especially for emerging playwrights, these paths generally require a great deal of research, tenacity, and resilience.

Established playwrights are sometimes commissioned by theatre companies to write or adapt plays specifically for those theatres. In this model the theatre usually pays a fee to the playwright in advance to develop the work. Often, but not always, a commissioned play will receive some sort of workshop experience as described in chapter six, and because the play is cultivated through a workshop process and receives at least one production, it is often well-positioned to be revised for publication or further productions.

Of course most plays are not commissioned and emerging playwrights are less likely to have such opportunities. Playwrights at all levels may have their work discovered by potential producers through festivals or NPD opportunities. These events generally attract directors and other theatre leaders who may see a play they feel fits the mission and aesthetic sensibility of their theatre. The producer may then approach the author of that play to negotiate its inclusion in an upcoming season.

Finally, some (though not many) theatre companies accept unsolicited script submissions. At most large companies, submissions are accepted only through a literary agent or when recommended by the artistic director of another established company. Several theatre companies (including a number of industry leaders) will accept query letters, resumes, and/ or short writing samples. Almost all theatre companies post their policies related to script submission on their websites. Playwrights should strictly adhere to these guidelines if they hope to have their work considered.

Ultimately, like most things in the theatre world, success as a playwright is built on relationships. As Laurie Brooks comments: "If you can find a theatre that will produce your work, that's fortuitous. If you find a theatre that believes in you, that's fabulous." Mark Lutwak also explains the importance of relationships, while noting that this may have impact on a playwright's writing process:

> Write whatever you want, just don't assume you have a right to be produced. You need to find the producing partner that has access to the audience that is open to the work. You can't force adults to attend the theatre, and you certainly can't make them bring or send their kids. There is a great difference between the work of a playwright and the work of a producer. If you develop a relationship with a producing institution, then they can help you understand the needs of their particular audience. This may or may not impact the writing process. If you are open as writer, then anything you let in will impact your work. It may or may not do so in a manner that helps you get produced.

What artistic directors seek

While writing an excellent script is always essential for playwrights hoping to see their work produced, an understanding of the type of work being produced and sought by producers can help playwrights tailor their work to meet those expectations. This is not to say that every new play should be similar to those that already exist – but whether playwrights intend to write a work that harmonizes with much of the canon or one that challenges the norm, they must first know what that norm is. One of the best ways to determine this is, of course, to see a great deal of TYA, and to research what theatres around the country are producing. To understand producers' philosophical and practical reasons for building particular seasons, we asked myriad artistic directors and producers what they sought in plays for their seasons. We include a wide variety of responses here to illustrate that while there are some trends, no two theatres are seeking the exact same thing, and a play that one theatre would reject out-of-hand could be the perfect fit for another company. Playwrights should therefore carefully research each company to which they are considered submitting their work, including its mission statement, the plays it has produced for the past several seasons, etc. Of course, checking basic policies (such as whether or not the theatre will accept unsolicited submissions at all) is essential.

What do you look for in TYA plays when planning your season?

Olivia Aston Bosworth

"Our first consideration is our audience. In the heart of Midtown Atlanta, our patron base is diverse and incredibly smart. Both our adult and youth performances need to reflect our city in every way possible. Casting needs to be flexible, and content should be universal to our very young audience. We look for scripts with an experiential journey and a heart. If the audience isn't a partner in the journey, our team works to develop that relationship in rehearsals. Often we are most interested in scripts featuring dual languages. Our most successful productions in the past five years have presented our audiences with Spanish, Japanese, and even nonsense languages."

Michael J. Bobbitt

"Some of the decisions are cost of production, number of actors, marquee value, fundability and the balance/marriage of art and commerce. However, what I aspire to most of the time is a great story with interesting characters that our audiences can relate to. Additionally, I look for stories that are dramatized in an entertaining way. I should qualify this by stating that entertainment could/should be moving, emotional, sometimes silly, and fun. Mostly and ultimately, I aspire to find scripts that will allow us to create a long-lasting memorable experience, so that we can smack our audience over the head with great theatre. Hopefully, this will encourage them to want to become artists or, at the very least, lifelong arts supporters. What I steer away from are prescriptive and didactic scripts. I really don't like plays that are trying to solve a 'world's problem.' If the story is strong and the characters are relatable and the script is well dramatized, the audience will get the lesson because the character's 'world problem' is really the character's problem. Lastly, I'll say, the 'problem' of the character can be as simple as learning how to tie his shoelaces. If the story is strong and it is well dramatized, it can be an important and memorable theatrical experience."

Rachel Briley

"Because I work in a university, there are many factors that come into play when choosing the season. We have to consider the following questions: number of roles? *(more often than not, we have many more female actors than males, so gender factors in);* scenic requirements?; costume requirements?; special technical requirements? *(for all the design elements: is this play do-able within the context of our resources?);* title recognition? *(we need to sell tickets!);* running time? *(approximately one hour). In addition, our TYA shows are being cast and having designers assigned to them at the same time as all the other shows in our department's season, so if other shows are not able to cover certain categories (i.e., perhaps another show only provides opportunities for seven actors), the TYA show is often left having to pick up the pieces and 'make up' for that loss (so in the main stage slot, we often are forced to choose very large-cast shows). Essentially it boils down to number of roles, design elements, title recognition, and running time, but of course all of this is connected to our internal resources. (I hate to admit that title recognition comes into play, because I never thought I would let that happen, but wearing the hat of the producer, I have to think about it. We survive on our ticket sales, so appealing to the gatekeepers matters.)"*

Adam Burke

"A script will make it past the first read if it makes me feel something*. I believe in the power of empathy and I believe great theatre has the power and potential to engage an audience empathetically. If I don't care about the characters and their relationships, I won't consider producing it. When it gets to that point I start looking at two primary factors. The first is economic: how many actors does it take; does it call for special effects like flight; does it require musicians; does my marketing team think it will sell tickets? The second is a mix of intangible factors: will it resonate with my audience in some way; which age will it serve (baby, pre-K, early elementary, middle/upper elementary, middle school, teen) and do I have a need to fill with that audience; how does it serve my current artists?"*

Jeannine Coulombe

"First and foremost, any script we consider must be based on children's literature or existing stories. We commission two to four world premiere adaptations each season, some are musical adaptations and some are straight plays; some are developed with a group of young actors and some have a more traditional development process. It depends on the story and our vision of how we will put it onstage. For the last several years we have worked with a dance company in developing world premiere ballets of several children's books. Our new work always starts with asking, 'What stories do we want to tell?' and 'How do we want to tell them?' We try to find a balance in the season in subject matter, musical/straight play, audience age range, and new literature versus classic literature as well as existing scripts/ musicals and commissioned new work. When looking at existing script adaptations of

children's literature we look at the theatricality of the adaptation: is it a dramatic interpretation or is it just prose onstage? If it is a musical, is it compelling, memorable music? Does it work to move the story forward or does it hold it back? Does this adaption excite us? Can we see it on our stage in front of our audience? Or can we do the adaptation ourselves to fit what we envision. The other consideration for us when looking at a script deals specifically with adult actors playing child roles. We don't do that, so we always look at how many adult roles versus youth roles are required in any given script."

Julia Flood

"Our mission includes the phrase 'inspired by the intelligence and emotional wisdom of young people' and this weighs heavily in all choices for our season. What does the play have to say that either reflects or engages the minds and emotional lives of young people in our community? What are the specific issues that youth in our community are dealing with right now and how can this play help them to process the questions in their minds? How can we take our audience on a journey of imagination that can only happen in a theatrical setting? These are among the considerations that are foremost in my mind when looking at plays or potential development projects. Then, there are the practical considerations like cast size, complex or expensive design elements, whether or not the production needs to tour, and whether parents and teachers will be able to connect with the play."

Jeff Frank

"When choosing a script for our season, there are a few non-negotiable qualities for me: the story has to be compelling and worth telling, the script engaging and truthful, and it must absolutely respect the intelligence of our audience. Scripts that fail to do any of those things – no matter how popular the title – are eliminated from consideration. Where do those compelling stories come from? For us it is a mix of great literature, both classic and contemporary, and original stories – many of which emerge from our community's rich and varied history. We have an opportunity and a responsibility to encourage reading and to build literacy by exposing young people to exceptional literature, which has led us to develop scripts ranging from Treasure Island *to* The Thief Lore, *from* Nancy Drew *to* Gathering Blue. *In addition to these adaptations, we also look to tell original stories and find that as we work with our community we are discovering more and more remarkable stories to tell – like* Don't Tell Me I Can't Fly *based on the life and work of a local artist. These original works emerge from, and therefore, engage our audiences, in a more profound manner. This engagement is further enhanced by our commitment to age-appropriate casting. We have found that our audiences are more invested in the productions when actual young people are onstage. With this in mind, we produce scripts that have a young person's point of view front and center. I tend to shy away from scripts written specifically to be performed with adults playing the parts of young people. Finally, and most importantly, we want to share stories that will provoke reflection and discussion, stories that reflect the diversity of our*

community, and promote understanding and awareness and encourage empathy. We are not afraid of tackling difficult subject matter, but I also believe that our plays should point us toward the light. This doesn't mean tidy and happy endings, but rather plays that do suggest that, despite the many challenges we face in this world, there is reason to go on, there is reason to hope."

Lauren Jost

"We devise all of our performances within the company. We work with a core idea that is of particular interest to one or more of our artists, and devise materials and storylines around that idea. A good finished script will be open-ended, multisensory, incorporate both familiar and fantastical elements, and be developmentally appropriate for young children. Most importantly, a good TVY script will be investigating a question that very young children are asking about the world and be guided by exploration of that question, not answers. We try to incorporate a blend of presentational and interactive styles as well as a diversity of art forms (puppetry, storytelling, dance, physical theatre)."

Jenny Anne Koppera

"We start by looking for scripts with great stories, strong translations, and universal themes that we hope will intersect well with and yet still stretch our audiences. We seek plays that deepen our global connections in ways that are intriguing, enriching, and surprising for our audiences. We also love plays that allow for innovation and creative possibility for our company to develop and perform. Lastly, since we are a new and small company, we also select plays that can be accomplished with a limited number of actors and those that can potentially be toured with simple production values."

Michelle Kozlak

"We don't usually begin our process with a script (even a partial one). It usually starts with a rough outline, storyboard or page-long treatment. All of our shows are world premiere productions that we have commissioned, are geared for babies and young toddlers (ages 0–2) or for pre-school/kindergarten aged children (ages 2–5), and are nonverbal, featuring live music and/or sound effects. The most important factors we look at when commissioning a new piece are to make sure that the story will be clear and accessible to the audience, that the show will have a strong visual component (whether that be through the action onstage, set, props, costumes, colors onstage, etc.), and that it will be a sensory experience (sound, visual, and sometimes tactile when we bring props out to the audience). The shows must be gently interactive and about 20–30 minutes in length. Our productions have incorporated a variety of musical styles and different artistic disciplines."

Mary Rose Lloyd

"We look for shows that are smart and surprising, visually compelling and artistically cohesive; productions that reach different ages at different levels and can be enjoyed by kids and families. We never present anything that we don't enjoy as much as the child sitting next to us. Our season includes a wide variety of genres; everything from theatre to music, dance, circus, and puppetry. Each type of show receives the same qualities of scrutiny."

Mark Lutwak

"I seek work that: Does not talk down to its audience; is character-driven; rests on dramatic action, not exposition; is meaningful and important to its audience; and is at least as well-written as the best of professional theatre."

Jon Ludwig

"Popular titles are very important. We create most of our scripts in-house. A critical factor for choosing outside scripts is that they must be allowed to be adapted for the puppetry. This often means editing dialogue, pumping up the action, and deleting or combining some characters. After all, we have to build our cast from scratch."

Judy Matetzschk-Campbell

"I am always looking for a great story, a great child-like protagonist and real danger as well as real hope. When planning a season, I always look for those things first. That is the only kind of theatre I want to do. The only other thing that I think about is making sure I have at least one play in our season that really is going to be a good first theatre experience for pre-kindergarten students. They are becoming a larger and larger part of our audience so I want to always be sure that I program at least one production specifically for them."

Paul Mesner

"Regarding puppet theatre: does the script talk when it needs to and does it show when it should?"

David Morgan

"We work in a market-driven economy, so that greatly affects our show selection. While many of our foreign counterparts get to create new works and experiment with styles thanks to the government support they are fortunate to have, we tend to base our shows on quantifiable educational value. Shows that match the core curriculum for schools, since

most of our audience are students. As a result we focus on books and rarely tell original stories. It's easiest for the teachers to justify seeing a play based on a book they read in class. Over the past 20 years our audience has gotten considerably younger; that also affects our script selection. We trend much younger than we used to. We are more likely to produce shows based on picture books and early readers than we are to do something like The Giver which is for older kids. We have recently begun TVY programs to much success. This is another market-driven commodity but the interesting thing with this is you don't have to use books as source material. Since the kids don't read yet and its parents and not educators bringing kids to the show, they are more open to the value of the shared experience as opposed to the adhesion to the core curriculum."

Lisa Portes

"There are three main factors that go into our decision-making process when planning upcoming seasons: our mission, our audience, and our student body. Our mission is to produce work that reflects the urban, contemporary, and multi-ethnic experience of our core audience, Chicago's elementary school children. I first look for points of resonance with Chicago kids. The words 'Urban', 'Contemporary', and 'Multi-Ethnic' are taped to my computer during season planning. Also, we are a part of the regular season of The Theatre School at DePaul University, so we also look for work that can offer creative challenges to our acting, design, dramaturgy, stage management, and tech students. We produce our season in an old 1300-seat Broadway road-house with all the bells and whistles a space like that has. I look for productions that can fit the scale of the space and provoke wildly creative thinking from our actors and designers, cool study guide ideas for our dramaturgs and exciting technical challenges for our tech and stage management students. It's unlikely we will produce a four-person play, for example, or something that would best be served by minimalism. Which loops back to our audience – if we are going to provide potentially the first theatrical experience for a Chicago child, we are going to make sure it is spectacular!"

Jeffrey Revels

"The most important and maybe the only attribute is that the story is well told and/or is a story we want to share with our audiences. The length of the script (running time) is not an issue at our theatre. Luckily, our school systems do not limit us to an hour or less. We are fortunate to tell the stories in their totality. There are other attributes: cast size and gender of the protagonists. If we are doing six shows in a season, then the shows must balance small, medium, and large-cast sizes. We cannot do all large-cast shows for budgetary reasons, but we do not do all small-cast shows either, so a script can have any size cast it requires. The same thought process follows with the gender of the protagonist. We like to balance the season so that we do not have five shows anchored by a male protagonist and one with a

female protagonist. It is important to us that our audiences see themselves onstage so we try to balance the gender of the main characters. Of course, there are exceptions and titles that fulfill both male and female leads in the same show. Again, for any one script, the only attribute that is important is that the story is well told!"

David Saar

"It has to be a story that I have to share with my audiences! That pesky passion thing! The reasons for the passion are constantly different: a new fresh voice, a risky topic that I think kids are ready to face, or a beloved story that I want to be sure is a part of a kid's literary and cultural awareness. Lots of reasons, but the commonality is passion. That said, I must also include the financial reality of supporting a company of resident artists, and am always aware that if I am going to go out on an artistic limb, it needs to be supported by a sturdy trunk of stories that provide easier access for the general audience."

Janet Stanford

"I love a well-written script! But that can mean many different things: sometimes it means poetry in the language or witty, dynamic dialogue. Other times it means a strong visual aptitude for storytelling and imagery. What I always look for is great subject matter that appeals both to educators and parents who are, after all, the gatekeepers for TYA. I believe that a child protagonist is almost always essential, plus entertaining, bold or quirky characters who drive a compelling argument and make me care about what happens to them. I am also drawn to scripts that offer the potential for interesting staging; by that I mean everything from creative movement, to live music, masks, puppets, swordplay, video, or cultural elements like Flamenco, Belly Dancing, Hip-Hop, or Commedia dell Arte. Sometimes leaders in TYA must choose titles that have popular appeal but that does not mean that we have to produce them in a traditional fashion. We can always add stylistic elements that surprise and excite our audience about a different way of seeing even the most familiar story."

Pat Wilhelms

"We pick our season by choosing plays that have name recognition or fit the mission of our issue-based play. The script has to be able to be cast locally; we can't afford a play with a huge cast. I love a script that is smart, and that has a broad audience appeal. Puns, word-play, modern references are all fun even for the older audience members; I don't like to choose plays that are only enjoyable to little people. I love plays without happy endings but I can't afford to do them very often because audiences won't come. The same is true if we choose a play that nobody has heard of. It's unfortunate. We can't take a risk yet. So I look to see what kids are reading in each grade level at their school, and see if there is a great adaptation available."

Self-producing

At times, playwrights create strong scripts that, for various reasons, theatre companies are not yet willing to produce. Michelle Wright notes that the writing/production/publication process:

> Is so difficult for playwrights because many publishers aren't interested in representing a script until it has gone through production, and many theaters aren't interested in producing unpublished scripts. So what do you do with that wonderful script you just finished? I feel that a script really isn't ready to be published until it has gone through the production process; characters and dialogue that read well but fall flat on stage all get worked out through that process. So it's really crucial (though I know not easy) to find a way to get your work produced. Some writers have even turned to self-producing because this is so important.

As Wright mentions, some playwrights in these situations choose to completely self-produce their work. Below we explore what this entails.

By self-producing, we mean completing all of the tasks that would normally be completed by a theatre company or producer who was interested in presenting a script a playwright had developed. Among other things, this includes raising (or providing) all of the funds necessary for the production, hiring (or soliciting the volunteer services of) a creative and production team (director, designers, stage management, technicians), procuring spaces in which to rehearse and perform the show (which may or may not be the same space), and overseeing all marketing efforts for the production (or hiring someone to oversee these tasks). In other words, we use the term "self-producing" to mean personally *organizing and overseeing* all the details of a production, though not necessarily self-directing or inhabiting any specific role other than playwright/producer. We asked respondents:

Should playwrights consider self-producing their work? If so, how might they go about this?

Samantha Macher

> *"If there is a situation fraught with more peril and possibility than self-producing, I do not know what it is. First of all, you've usually put your own money, time, and professional contacts on the line for what some may say is a pipe dream. Second of all, these are your words and your hiring decisions, so if it's terrible, you have no one to blame but yourself. But, if it goes well, you may experience the artistic fulfillment and acclaim that one can only have from mounting a successful production. And accolades aside, there are a lot of advantages to this kind of production. The primary rewards are really pronounced, at least for me, in the development stage. To be honest I love self-producing in this phase of my work.*

It allows me as an artist to try new things with my text without being beholden to another producer's financial commitments. Because it's my money and my time, I can make reasonable adjustments nimbly and easily. So long as I am respectful of others, I can request a line change on the fly or make executive decisions in regard to the look or feel of the show if appropriate.

Working with young actors, though, can be a little more challenging in respect to major changes. Because they don't have a lengthy history with making huge adjustments on a dime, you'll need to be cognizant of how making the text work for you might mean a lot of stress for them. Another disadvantage to mounting one's own production is that you often don't give yourself enough space to really worry about one job. When a theatre company produces your play, your only responsibility is to ensure the quality and integrity of the text. When you assume the role of producer, one may find that their responsibility to the text is sacrificed for the finances, or other looming challenges, which will inevitably come up in production.

To avert these destructive distractions, I would suggest that your text be as close to stage-ready as possible. I recommend spending a lot of time interviewing and hiring the right people for your play. Find passionate people with a great track record. Though there's no failsafe against making the wrong hiring decisions, I will say that the time you invest in this is almost more important than the time you spend crafting the play. I cannot stress this enough: if you do not have the right people in place, do not proceed with the production."

John Newman

"I believe that a playwright can effectively direct, and even produce, her/his own adaptation of book because the processes of directing and adaptation are similar. Both adapting and directing involve interpreting the text and restructuring it into a theatrical language that communicates to an audience. On the other hand, I would advise a playwright against directing or producing his/her original play, as the individual would have to create and interpret the same text. A well-rounded and multidimensional play production requires at least two distinct perspectives. In an adaptation, the perspective of the author is distinctive from the playwright/director while in an original work, the perspective of the playwright and the director are one and the same. Just as two eyes are required for dimensional vision, two perspectives are required for dimensional theatre."

Pam Sterling

"At my university and I think at many others, there is a student-run theatre company that offers students opportunities to produce their own work, including new plays by student playwrights. The playwrights do not entirely self-produce. They do get support from the student staff, but a lot of times they end up having to find their own designers, cast members, and certainly do a lot of their own marketing. This process greatly encourages and builds the entrepreneurship skills that all theatre artists need to have, which is good. However, the

playwright can become so enmeshed in the peripheral activities of selling and marketing their play, they can lose sight of doing the development work that any new play emphatically needs in early productions. However, often it is necessary for a playwright to 'self-produce' a workshop or a staged reading of his play in order to first hear it with voices other than his own. I have done this myself, and usually encourage new playwrights to go ahead and produce 'table reads,' staged readings, or workshops themselves and not wait around for a theatre to offer them one."

Getting published

While a playwright might choose never to publish her work, but rather to have her agent represent the work (or even do this herself), publication is often an eventual goal. In the section below, respondents speak to when (if ever) playwrights should pursue publication, how they can determine to which publishers it might be appropriate to submit their work, and what publishers might expect from playwrights. As discussed earlier, few plays are published unless they have first been produced. Pam Sterling notes: "There are no publishers that I am aware of that will publish a script by a new writer that has not had a proven track record of at least 2 or 3 full productions."

When, if at all, in the play development process should a playwright pursue having her work published? Are there circumstances in which it might be more advantageous for a playwright not to publish a particular script?

Sandy Asher

"While publication does bring with it a kind of approval and permanence – and maybe even the illusion of immortality – it's really all about marketing. The publisher has to feel there will be interest in the script beyond the originating production. A lot of interest. Publishing is a business. Respect and admiration don't always add up to marketability. Some plays lend themselves to publication and some don't. A play may have a universal theme, but may not have reproducible characters or action. If it was built on certain actors to perform for certain audiences under very particular circumstances, that may be where it needs to stay. Plays that have broad applications are more likely to appeal to a publisher. In that case, a playwright would be wise to follow rules set down a long time ago by Anchorage Press: before publication, a play should have three different productions with three different directors, none of whom are the playwright. There are always exceptions to this rule, but it provides useful guidelines. Only fresh, objective eyes can tell you if you've set down on the page everything you need for others to understand what you meant. It's a slow process, but a necessary one. And while helping the playwright revise, clarify, and polish the script, those productions will also help convince a publisher that the play has legs."

Jonathan Dorf

"First off, before you even start looking, make sure your play is ready. Plays for young audiences can get published without reviews or even productions, but I think it's important to make sure your play is road-tested first. Not everything that appears to work on the page actually works onstage, and the only way to find that out is in production. So take the time to find that production (or productions), because once your play is published, nobody's going to allow you to send in a rewrite. Also, particularly since first impressions are so important, you don't want to send a publisher something that's not your strongest work."

Larissa Fasthorse

"I've only pursued publishing after a play has been produced. I've been asked to submit an unproduced script, but I didn't because this is a collaborative form. Without the input of development, directors, dramaturgs, designers, actors, and audience, it's not finished for me."

Barry Kornhauser

"Although not a guarantee of any sort, having a play published is perhaps the best means of seeing the work given multiple productions. But for the sake of the play, it is perhaps wise not to rush into publication. A general rule of thumb is for a new work to have a few productions before being considered by a publisher. This is a good idea because it offers the playwright the opportunity to learn what works and what doesn't on the stage. The caveat to this, of course, is that those few productions are strong ones, luminously translating the words on the page to the stage, and that the playwright takes an active part in that process, while getting to stick around at least a little while beyond the rehearsal period to observe that final acid-test of validation, audience response. While no two audiences are alike, the response of any is likely to be at least a bit informative. So it is advantageous to be patient about publishing. The act of publication has the effect of incising your words in granite, so you want to be sure they're saying all you want them to say in the precise way you would like them spoken. I have a good many plays, some quite old now, that I have not yet submitted for publication because I think that given the time and opportunity (both far too rare), I'd still like to try to make better."

Anne Negri

"When I began writing my first full-length TYA play, With Two Wings, *I could not even conceive of publishing my play. I needed to write it first, then someone had to find it interesting enough to either develop or produce it. Those seemed like big enough goals early on for my play. However, after a few years, workshop productions, development opportunities, a world premiere, and a few productions under my belt, it felt like* With Two Wings *was done. When I watched productions I didn't cringe, wince, or scribble intensely*

131

in a notebook anymore. It felt like a finished play and I didn't want to change anything more. Fortuitously, I had shared early drafts of the play with a publisher who had been following my play's trajectory over the years, and she contacted me with an interest in publishing With Two Wings *exactly when I was feeling 'done.' With my publisher, I no longer have to negotiate individual contracts with theatre companies and it has a broader exposure and accessibility in their catalogue of plays. I work full-time, so it was also a relief to have someone else take care of my play.*

There are definitely scenarios where it might be advantageous for a playwright to delay publication of a play or not publish their play. Once a play is published, the publishing company retains a percentage of the proceeds of sales of individual plays and future royalties for productions. If a playwright has the luxury of getting to be a full-time playwright, they may have the time to devote to promoting/sending out their play to theatres all over the country and really marketing their work. If a play has the potential to be popular and produced by many companies, a playwright might wait to publish so that the publishing company would not take a percentage. The full amount of each negotiated contract would go directly to the playwright. Some playwrights have enough success that they can hire an agent. An agent would also need a percentage. In addition, a company may have commissioned or invested in a play and have negotiated a percentage of the proceeds of that play for a certain time period. So, if a playwright has to give a percentage of a royalty to a publisher, an agent, and potentially a producing organization, then their take home amount becomes less and less. In the end, playwrights have to decide how comfortable they feel with their play going out into the world, how much a publisher might give their play a wider audience, and how much they want to manage their work on their own."

Pam Sterling

"I would advise new playwrights to become aware of the resources provided by the Dramatists Guild. Each year the Guild publishes a Resource Directory *that lists hundreds of theatres with their submission guidelines; deadlines, formatting, whether they accept plays for young audiences or unsolicited manuscripts, what kinds of topics of genre of script they may be looking for, etc. The* Resource Directory *usually includes information about the technical challenges of certain theatres, as well as casting requirements. Playwrights need to understand they have to do most of the marketing of their script, including sending invitations to performances or sending reviews, to get the attention of a publisher or an artistic director."*

How can a TYA playwright go about finding an appropriate publisher for a particular script?

Matt Buchanan

"Ideally, you want a play that's mostly going to appeal to high school drama teachers looking for a competition play to be placed with a publisher that focuses on that market, and a play

that's mostly going to appeal to the volunteer directing the middle school play to be with a publisher most of them will know about. But it's not so easy to figure out who's who. All I can suggest is that you order all of the catalogues, and, to the extent that you can afford to, read representative works from various publishers. I suppose you could choose a publisher and try to write the kind of play they tend to like, but I've never been able to bring myself to do that. I write the kind of play I want to write and then try to pick the best place to send it – either the publisher I think is most likely to accept it or the publisher I think is most likely to be able to sell it well. (Unfortunately, the very best publishers of works for young audiences mostly won't even look at a script that has not had a 'first class' professional production, which lets out all of us who intentionally write for young performers.)

You also have to decide where the balance is between your need to make money and your sense of artistic integrity. I personally avoid a number of publishers because the quality of their scripts overall is poor. I don't like the idea of my work being tarred with the same brush, which is probably snobbish of me, and I don't like to think of my work being produced by the sort of clueless amateur who would shop from those catalogues. But at least two of the publishers in this category are enormously profitable because of their ubiquity – their catalogues are the ones most likely to be familiar to teachers with no formal theatre training. I'd probably make a little more money if I placed my work there – but I can't bring myself to do it."

Jonathan Dorf

"Spend some time getting to know a publisher's holdings by browsing their website/catalogue. Does your play seem like a fit? For example, if they focus on the high school market, they may not be the best place for your elementary school musical. While it may seem like a good idea to be their only elementary musical, unless they're planning a big push into that market, people aren't going to come to them for that type of play, leaving your latest opus stranded. Further, do you recognize any of their authors? Do you like the idea of being in their company? If you actually know any of their writers, ask them about their experience. While publishers are really more there to market the brand than a particular play, assuming they've accepted your play and you're weighing whether to sign, see what they think the target market is for your play, and if that makes sense to you. How do they market their plays? Do they have a catalogue? Go to conferences?"

Joanna Kraus

"In the last few years several long-established and distinguished companies have sadly closed while a few new ones have popped up. But there are still stellar publishers. Look at their catalogues. See what they publish in children's theatre. You can be assured that they won't want duplicates to compete with what they already publish (i.e., it's unlikely they'd want five versions of the same folk or fairy tale). I believe it's best to send a query with a brief synopsis of your script, its production history and awards, and brief biographical data. Keep in mind that what one publisher may not want might fit another house perfectly."

Greg Romero

"I've only approached one publisher, and am fortunate enough to have developed a good relationship with them. I originally approached them because I was aware of the company's owners, and through mutual friends and colleagues' reports, they were quality, hard-working people. I took a look at their authors and the kinds of plays they were publishing, the company's mission and goals, and found that these were people and stories and an approach to publishing that I could believe in and that my own work and way of working might match well with them. I also contacted a couple of their authors who I knew personally, and when they told me they were enjoying their experience, the decision to send my work to them became easy and I feel very fortunate that they have liked my writing."

Michelle Wright

"Check the submission policies for all of the major publishers out there. Plays for Young Audiences (PYA) primarily represents plays and musicals originally commissioned and/or produced by either Seattle Children's Theatre or the Children's Theatre Company in Minneapolis. Occasionally PYA will consider representing other works of PYA playwrights or works recommended by an artistic director, literary manager, or dramaturg affiliated with a professional theatre. We regret that we are unable to accept unsolicited manuscripts."

What factors affect publishers' decision-making processes when determining if they should publish particular scripts?

Jonathan Dorf

"The quality of the script is always number one. I don't care who the author is or what it's about – if we don't read it and say: 'We really like this,' we're not taking it. Sometimes that means having to reject scripts from authors we already publish, or on topics about which we want to have scripts (e.g., bullying). But even very good scripts get rejected. Why? One big reason is that it's too close to something we already have. It may be that it's an Alice in Wonderland *adaptation, and given that we already publish a pair of excellent adaptations, it would have to be something extraordinary and very different to consider adding to the catalogue.*

The other big question is: 'can we market this?' That usually has to do with three areas: content, casting (size, gender breakdown/flexibility), and running time. Adult content, for example, has to be approached thoughtfully. We love plays with challenging ideas or that embrace theatricality, but things like profanity or overt sexual situations don't sit well with most youth producers. When it comes to casting, schools tend to like large and/or flexible casts with lots of girls, so if a play is mostly guys, we'll have to think long and hard about whether there's a market for it. Of course, small casts may be great for some groups, whether those are smaller schools or professional companies with touring shows.

It's ultimately about whether the cast works for the type of show it is. Do we take it knowing that nobody may be able to produce it? Sometimes, if we're passionate about the play and its subject matter, we'll roll the dice and hope they come up lucky sevens. But sometimes we'll tell the author that we really enjoyed the work, but we don't feel that we can market this particular one successfully. Finally, when we agree to publish someone's work, we're both committing to a relationship. The author needs to be comfortable with us, and we need to be comfortable with the author. From our end, that means being satisfied that the author will be a supportive, positive partner in the publishing and marketing process."

Steve Fendrich

"For Pioneer Drama Service, we discuss the quality and will it be a good fit. Is there a spot in our catalogue for it? How different is it from our other shows? Cast size? We are always looking for 'wholesome' shows that will be embraced by communities. From a business point of view, the best-selling shows are the traditional tales. Alice in Wonderland, Snow White, *and* Sleeping Beauty *will always be popular. For a playwright, that makes it very difficult to get published since every publishing company has an adaptation of the story. Unless there is an intriguing twist in the story, it usually will not stand a chance of getting published. That means that writers have to find a unique twist to these traditional stories. Thus, 'fractured fairy tales' have become very big.*

As for shows that are targeted for middle schools and high schools, Pioneer looks at them both. However, our company has found that our social awareness plays (e.g., drug abuse, suicide, etc.) do not do well. Our shows are targeted for a typical drama club: more females than males, sets that can be simple (or made to be elaborate), and running times that vary but don't go over 90 minutes. We want our shows to be fun and wholesome. Getting a play published by a company can be extremely difficult. We publish about one percent of the plays that have been submitted. The next step is finding a group that would like to put it on. It's not only competing against other shows within the publishing/licensing company, but going against thousands of other shows in the other major publishing companies."

Michelle Wright

"The plays in the Plays for Young Audiences (PYA) catalogue have been curated by an artistic team of literary managers and artistic directors, so the PYA catalogue is reflective of those artistic choices. I am very proud that we represent a diverse array of playwrights, some of whom have never written for young audiences before, all with unique voices, and artistic and political sensibilities. All of the plays in the PYA catalogue have been produced by a professional theatre."

***

This chapter reviewed how playwrights might go about having their work produced and published, but these are only the first steps in ensuring a play's longevity. The next chapter introduces the topic of marketing to explore how playwrights might promote themselves and their work.

Chapter 8

Marketing and Promotion

The last chapter explored how a playwright might go about getting their work produced or published. It is important to remember that even once these benchmarks have been reached, his work promoting their material is never done. Even the best agent will not be able to identify every possible opportunity, and while publishers naturally seek to have playwrights' work produced, it would be unwise to rely primarily on their efforts to keep his work alive. With perhaps a few exceptions, most writers need to actively contribute to the marketing of their work throughout their entire career. In this chapter we explore how playwrights can develop and nurture strong reputations for themselves and their body of work along with if and when to pursue agent representation.

Personal marketing

Experts in many fields say it all the time: Network. Market yourself. For many people this can be a distressing process. Regardless, a playwright must take risks in order to achieve success, and fortunately there are organic ways to establish himself.

The best way for a playwright to make his presence known in the field is to actively participate in it. Artistic directors, publishers, literary managers, and others looking for new plays and new voices are much more likely to put a play on top of their reading pile if it is by someone they personally know and respect. Key ways that playwrights can establish themselves are to submit to NPD opportunities/contests and submit for awards. Playwrights who win awards or are chosen for NPD opportunities are likely to become better known as artists, collaborators, and contributors to the larger conversation. Appendices C and D include select listings of these opportunities, but playwrights should also do their own research. Even if a playwright's work isn't chosen for a particular conference or event, he should still attend if possible to listen, learn, and familiarize himself with current trends in the field. It is much easier to meet people naturally in such settings when one doesn't feel everything is hinged upon forging connections. Nevertheless, playwrights should always have business cards on hand (with their professional website listed) and be prepared to send out their best work if asked.

One avenue for playwrights who would like to have their work for young performers produced is to build relationships with local drama teachers. If they do not already know one (or have a possible personal connection to one), playwrights might send query letters to local drama teachers, or call schools to see if there are any available with whom they can speak. Playwrights can also attend regional and national drama education conferences, such as those held by the Educational Theatre Association (EdTA) or American Alliance for Theatre and Education (AATE) or search online to see if there is an organization in their region or state.

Playwrights without the resources to go to conferences and events independently, as well as those who wish to supplement face-to-face experiences, can still be involved in the community from home. Web-based platforms, such as the New Play Exchange and Write Local, Play Global, give playwrights the opportunity to share their work and perspectives and learn about others' work in the community. Professional organizations such as Dramatist's Guild, TYA/USA (The US center for ASSITEJ International), and AATE allow members to build personal profiles on their websites. Other examples of organizations and forums that can assist playwrights are listed in Appendix B.

We asked respondents for their perspectives on the importance of personal marketing:

How can playwrights help develop a strong reputation for their body of work? Is it important for a playwright to develop a personal "brand" or "market himself" as a playwright for young audiences?

Jonathan Dorf

"Writing a great play is only half the battle. Without proper marketing, a play is like a tree falling in the forest with no one to hear it, and this is just as true in the world of young audiences as it is elsewhere in the playwriting world. In some ways, it may be even more important, because so much material for young audiences demonstrates a complete lack of understanding of the target group. If you can create and promote a brand that solidifies your position as someone who not only writes good plays but also understands the needs of young actors and audiences, people will begin to understand that they can look to you for work to produce in this arena.

What, practically speaking, does this sort of branding look like? On my website I have a specific section called 'Teen Favorites' to promote my plays for teens, as well as a collection of teen monologues and scenes meant to draw traffic and provide me with another avenue to promote the plays from which they come. If you've produced one of my plays, I want you to know about the other ones. As part of that marketing effort, I maintain an email list and send out regular emails with a heavy emphasis on my work for teens, and my Facebook fan pages and Twitter feed also skew in that direction. I try to stay active in a number of drama teacher/youth-centric e-groups as well. And perhaps most important, some years ago, I co-founded YouthPLAYS, a publishing company focused on plays for young people, which gave me an even stronger voice in the TYA conversation.

The flip side of being a playwright who focuses on TYA – and branding yourself that way – is that sometimes those who write for youth are dismissed as somehow 'less than' those who write for adults. It's no easier to write a great play for young people than it is to write one for older ones. In fact, it may be harder, given the honesty of young audiences. But if you plan to work in multiple genres/markets, then it's incumbent upon you to market yourself strongly in each."

Finegan Kruckemeyer

"In my experience, it is a form of pigeon-holing (not necessarily in a bad sense) that is bestowed upon you. Our sector does in some ways exist on a perceived periphery – theatre companies having an umbrellaed education programme, funding bodies having a separate youth pool, awards nights having a specific TYA category – and if you elect to write for this sector long enough, then others will view that as your prerogative.

This can be wonderful, in terms of one's plays circulating widely in what is a broad and collegial network, in terms of good houses owing to a societal permission for going to the theatre when young. And eventually, whether focused on self-branding or not, a brand will form around your body of plays.

At that point, it is to every writer's discretion as to how they respond. Personally, I've embraced it, as I love the community, the discipline, and the breadth of TYA.

Thematically, I love the skirting of taboo (large, human, emotional themes rather than illicit ones). Poetically, I love the way language is celebrated by TYA audiences and producers both, allowing words to become a game in themselves. Practically, I had lovely friends build me a website which sought to aesthetically evoke a play's tone. Actively, I travel to the countries where my plays sometimes reside, but always write the words at home, in a place that is familiar and removed from any notions of industry. Nostalgically, I appeal to the memory of what I loved as a child. But artistically, I seek to write plays that can be accessed by all.

All of this is cultivating my work's initial 'branded' perception, I suppose. But then I only remain excited about this discipline by actively seeking to write ever new things, and not perpetually mine the old – with the latter, both the brand and the man would struggle."

Janet Stanford

"I would say that your work is your brand. No form of marketing or self-promotion can substitute for the quality and character of the writing. Artistic relationships are all about aesthetic compatibility in my experience. Our taste as artists is what defines us and getting to know who you are aligned with can be helpful to a young writer as she grows into her own voice. Writers could generally do more to familiarize themselves with the kind of work that's being done around the country and try to match themselves with theatres where they feel their work belongs. That said, it is always valuable to attend conferences and new play development workshops, do playwright slams, and keep in touch with directors whose work you like."

Pam Sterling

"Even after a play is published the playwright still needs to make the extra effort to make sure potential producers are aware of his/her script. The publishers will put it in their

catalogue and will do some marketing, but the playwright cannot assume that the publisher will do it all. Some publishers have over 1000 scripts in their catalogue and cannot exhaustively market them all."

Pat Wilhelms

"I don't look to see if a playwright writes specifically for young audiences. I only look for a great script that I think my community would like. I do pay attention to winners of competitions in the field and when a colleague tells me about a play that has been fantastic, but that is by no means my only criteria. It is always wonderful when a playwright visits the theatre producing their play. It certainly establishes a relationship that could mean producing more plays in the future."

Michelle Wright

"If you are currently 'self-representing', start a website, join organizations in the field, and list your work online. Use social media to promote your work as much as possible."

Agent representation

While many established TYA playwrights are represented by agents, others are not. Whether or not an agent would benefit any given playwright depends on a variety of factors, often (but not always) related to where he is in his playwriting career. We asked respondents:

When should playwrights for young audiences pursue agent representation?

Roxanne Schroeder-Arce

"I have never felt the need for an agent."

Dennis Foon

"You need an agent to negotiate contracts. If you don't have a contract, an agent isn't going to do you a ton of good."

D.W. Gregory

"Even though an agent technically works for you, the reality is they pick and choose their clients. If you have an agent you'll be taken more seriously and your work will be read, but there's no guarantee that your career will take off as a result. Certainly if you're working in professional TYA theatres, you want an agent representing you."

Susan Gurman

"A playwright should pursue representation when working with a theatre or other producer and needs the advice, promotion, and guidance of an agent."

Y York

"The playwright, especially a new writer, needs to understand the business end of things. An agent can help with that. You get the agent by getting work. That guy who won't take your call suddenly will when you have a contract you'd like him to review (for his ten percent fee). Also, if you have a production in a town in which the agency resides, you can invite the agent to the production. Look at the client list; that should tell you if you're a good fit."

***

How can playwrights pursue agent representation?

Even once a playwright decides he is ready for an agent, the process of finding one is not easy and can take some time. Singer advises: "Keep in mind that the number of experienced theatre agents is relatively small in comparison with the number of writers seeking representation" (195). Though this may seem discouraging, the key is for a playwright to stay focused on his craft, learn as much as he can about managing his career, be involved in the field, and be ready if and when opportunities arise.

Below are some suggestions for playwrights who would like to pursue agent representation:

- Research TYA playwrights whose work seems similar to their own; look at their websites to see who represents them. If possible, talk to them about their relationships with their agents.
- Talk with playwrights represented by particular agencies and artistic directors or other professionals familiar with the field for personal recommendations and/or to facilitate introductions.
- Consult the Dramatist's Guild *Resource Directory Online* (access is limited to Guild members).

Suggestions for additional resources can be found through organizations and texts listed in Appendices A and B.

Once a playwright identifies an agency he feels would be a good fit, he should research the agency's policies for potential clients. For example: is the agency open to accepting query letters and submissions? If so, the playwright should follow the agency's guidelines without exception. He should ensure anything he submits is presented professionally. This includes having it thoroughly proofed for errors, using professional stage play script formatting (e.g., those available in Final Draft or The Playwright's Center's downloadable MS Word template). The submission should represent not only the playwright's best work but also his awareness of the agency's aesthetics and needs. If an agency does not post detailed guidelines, Appendix A includes texts and organizations that also offer templates and in-depth advice.

If the agency only accepts personal recommendations, playwrights should consider whether they know an artistic director, literary manager, or other notable professional who could make that introduction. Alternatively, another playwright already represented by the agency might be willing to make a recommendation. If a playwright procures a meeting with a potential agent, he should research the agency thoroughly in advance and be familiar with the plays and authors it represents. He should also read trade publications regularly in order to be able to participate in an informed manner during the meeting.

While finding even a single agent can be difficult, some playwrights may find that they have multiple agencies interested in representing them. Dennis Foon suggests when courting a potential agent, a playwright should, "have coffee and get a feeling for the person. Do you like them? Do they seem human? Do you like/respect the other writers represented by the agency? If you can, talk to other writers the agent represents and see how they feel about them."

We asked respondents about what happens after a playwright has procured an agent:

What should playwrights expect from an agent in terms of support and services?

Dennis Foon

"I've had a lot of agents over the years and have found they do very little in terms of promotion or getting commissions. One thing a good agent can do for you is open doors; set up meetings for you with producers and directors. That's something that can be hard to get on your own."

D.W. Gregory

"Agents generally don't get you work. They can certainly submit your plays around, and a good agent will help you work out a plan for that and a plan for the work you ought to pursue. But you still have to do a lot of legwork yourself and make connections where you can. Most productions are going to come out of those relationships."

Susan Gurman

"An agent-playwright relationship is akin to a professional marriage: each must work with the other. Each must be respectful and informative. The agent works on the playwright's behalf to both secure work, to negotiate contracts, and to promote the client."

Y York

"While an agent will submit your play, you are still the best advocate for your work. Getting an agent shouldn't mean you stop your own play promotion. You and the agency work together with the same goal of getting your play read and produced widely. Respect your

agent's time; you are not the only client, but your calls and communications should be returned. Your agent receives your fees and sends you a check minus the agency commission; have a firm understanding of how and when the checks are sent. Your agent has more connections than you do, but it is always your play that lands the gig."

***

In short, having an agent doesn't mean a playwright can afford to stop spending time and resources on the business side of his work. Ultimately, with or without an agent, playwrights are best served by becoming proficient at managing their own careers.

In this chapter, we touched upon the importance of marketing oneself, of committing time to learning the ins and outs of managing one's own career, and provided an overview of issues related to agent representation. In the next chapter we discuss whether it is possible to make a living as a TYA playwright.

Chapter 9

Income Potential

Anyone who has worked in the arts knows that one of the biggest pragmatic challenges is finding a way to support herself as an artist. This is especially true for TYA playwrights. Unless playwrights are extremely fortunate, have well-placed connections, and write scripts with mass commercial capacity (e.g., *Seussical*), their earning potential writing TYA is very limited. Even playwrights who do have such resources still often face great struggle from a financial standpoint. The comments regarding adaptations in chapter five apply equally to the larger market; hope for profit is an extremely ill-advised reason to pursue this work. Playwrights must be resilient, resourceful, business-savvy, tenacious, graceful, talented, hard-working, and a bit lucky to generate income from their work. Even then they should not anticipate a financial windfall. To best equip playwrights with a realistic picture of the field, what they might anticipate as income from playwriting, and to offer ideas about complementary jobs and careers, we asked various respondents for their perspectives on earning a living in (and outside of) the field.

Can one make a living as a TYA playwright?

Sandy Asher

"As Robert Anderson, of Tea and Sympathy *fame, once said: 'You can make a killing in the theater, but not a living.' 'A living' implies a steady income, and there's nothing steady about a life in the arts, at least not in this country. Perhaps a few people have payrolled jobs as playwrights-in-residence at theatres that can pay a living wage, but that would be highly unusual. For the rest of us, it's a constant roller coaster ride – at best. We write what we have to write, and hope for the best. But don't expect to 'earn a living as a playwright for young audiences.'"*

Matt Buchanan

"The short answer is no, sadly. I neither know personally, nor know of a single playwright who supports him/herself entirely by writing plays for youth. I have no proof that such people don't exist, but I've never heard of them. It's even less likely if you focus on writing plays for young performers – those are never going to be picked up by a professional company and then moved to Broadway, which is at least theoretically possible with a play intended for professional children's theatre."

Laurie Brooks

"If you're in the field to make money, you are likely to be disappointed."

Jonathan Dorf

"Making a living as a playwright is tough, regardless of whether you're writing for young people or for adults. In the youth world, unless you're writing shows that have regular runs at flagship TYA companies and other professional theatres, you're generally making your money in volume. In other words, you probably aren't getting that much money for each production (much of the time it might be only $50 or $100), so you have to have quite a few productions to make money. And realistically, unless you've got a really hot script or a whole lot of plays that get done quite regularly, you're not going to do quite enough volume to live off of it."

Dennis Foon

"Theatre is a precarious business, and it's even trickier for TYA artists."

José Cruz González

"It is difficult for any playwright to make a living in the American Theatre. Playwrights have to find a way to support their writing."

Dwayne Hartford

"There may be TYA playwrights who make their living solely from playwriting, but I don't know of any."

Joanna Kraus

"In my experience, with some exceptions, it's virtually impossible to make a living writing plays for youth. Theatre, in general, has always been a precarious profession with regard to income. Theatre for youth with its low royalties, low ticket prices, is at the bottom of the scale. If you can also write for film and television the answer would be, yes, you can possibly make a living. But no guarantees."

Mark Lutwak

"Nobody earns a living as a playwright for youth. Even those widely produced playwrights for youth cobble together a living from a range of sources."

***

What are some ways (e.g., complimentary careers, etc.) to make ends meet, while still carving out time for writing?

Laurie Brooks

"I was Assistant Professor at New York University where I taught playwriting and TYA during the first ten years of my career. Through that association, I developed a number of my plays at the NYU Provincetown Playhouse New Plays for Young Audiences."

Matt Buchanan

"The most obvious answer is to teach. Most of the top children's playwrights in the United States also teach playwriting or children's theatre at the college level. You can even make a living teaching in a primary or secondary school. I think it's pretty clear that teaching is the most common source of income for Youth Theatre artists. While this works well for some, it has two serious problems: first, for a dedicated teacher, the job tends to become all-encompassing, especially at the pre-college level, and especially for drama teachers. When I was working regularly as a school drama teacher I was unable to stop myself from putting in truly insane hours on the job. As a result, I did not have the time I needed to write. The second problem is less a problem for the artist than for his/her students. Personally, I was a teacher before I was a playwright and I truly enjoyed teaching and was enriched by it, but not every artist who pays the bills by teaching can say that. For the sake of our kids, I would strongly urge you not to choose teaching as a way of supplementing your playwriting income unless you truly have that missionary zeal for teaching.

What I have chosen to do lately is to find jobs that I don't fundamentally care much about. For me, that's really the only way I can avoid taking my work home with me. I do my job at work to the best of my ability because that's just who I am, but when my shift is over I leave, regardless of any pending projects or deadlines – as long as I know I'm doing my best, my conscience is clear. Thus I'm able to confine the job totally within its prescribed hours, and the rest of my time is mine to use for my art, without a single brain cell being wasted worrying about the job. I have managed a toy store. I have worked as an audio-visual technician for corporate events. I have worked as a night watchman. Currently I deliver newspapers in the middle of the night. Ironically, any one of these jobs would be utterly soul-killing if I regarded them as careers, but that's exactly what makes them ideal as ways to pay the bills so I can write – and I believe my writing is of substantial value to the world.

This approach currently works for me, but it has its drawbacks. The kinds of jobs that one can leave entirely in the office are almost invariably low paying. I'm able to make it work because, firstly, I've reached a point in my writing career where I actually do make some real money, so I don't need a job that pays all of the bills, and, secondly, I have extremely modest financial needs, since I'm not supporting a family, have no expensive hobbies, and am generally comfortable being poor. Plus, there are social consequences. When someone asks what I do for a living, I'm perfectly comfortable answering 'I'm a playwright and a composer,' because that's exactly what I am, but

I can't bring anyone to my home without exposing myself as a penniless one. I know playwrights who work as script consultants for film, television, or theatre. If you have the temperament for such work, that's a real option. We're all different, and different things will work for us."

Maggie-Kate Coleman

"I am fortunate to be employed as a theatre educator as well."

Jonathan Dorf

"Personally, I do some teaching and script consulting, and YouthPLAYS, my publishing company, is just starting to get past the start-up phase and hopefully will start to generate more income. Some lucky writers work in film or TV, while still others do copywriting or work in literary management or work in other theatre jobs (for example, they may also be actors). And many, many people teach, either at the college or K-12 level. Of course, some writers simply go with subsistence 9–5 jobs that have a finite daily endpoint, after which they can devote themselves entirely to their writing."

Dennis Foon

"I've always had to multitask to survive, writing in many genres. Day jobs can be onerous if they steal from your writing time. On the less demanding side, Quentin Tarrantino worked in a video store for years, and many writers have had jobs in libraries and bookstores. But if you have a vocation that inspires you or gives you background knowledge that will pay off in dividends with a writing career, I don't see the problem. A lot of former cops, teachers, lawyers, and spies work as TV writers. That being said, playwrights are a special breed. We need to know all aspects of theatre – acting, directing, and production. And it's even more specialized with TYA. I was Artistic Director of Green Thumb Theatre for 12 years and it taught me a ton. So if you can find some kind of job in the theatre, any job, it would be invaluable."

José Cruz González

"Some teach, others work in television or film, while others have jobs that can be flexible so they have time to write. I've been fortunate to teach playwriting at a university. That job has underwritten my writing."

D.W. Gregory

"I would expect that teaching, acting, directing could be complementary paths that one could use to put together a living in Youth Theatre, but it's not the path I'm on. I have always had outside jobs, always in editing or writing. I came to writing plays rather late in life, but it never worked out for me to leave full-time employment to focus on playwriting."

Dwayne Hartford

"While commissions and royalties are a great supplement to my income, I doubt I would ever have enough productions going consistently to make playwriting my sole source of income. It

seems that many TYA playwrights work for theatre companies or teach at universities. It certainly is a challenge to earn a living and to find the time and energy to devote to writing. This has been a struggle for me personally, as I am not the most disciplined of writers, and my other work duties, directing and acting, do require much energy and attention. I am fortunate, in that being a playwright in residence at Childsplay, I am given periods of time to concentrate on my writing. I am working on carving out more writing time outside of these writing periods."

Joanna Kraus

"Teaching is a viable solution with a steady, though not robust, income and its long summer break plus mid-semester vacations. In addition, there's freelance work such as writing reviews, magazine articles, and, if you are mobile, accepting residencies at different theatres and universities."

Generating money through playwriting

As indicated above, even the most successful playwrights nearly always rely upon income from other sources. Some do earn income from their writing, and some even earn relatively substantial sums. These earnings generally come in the form of royalties, commissions, playwriting-related grants and fellowships, and/or awards that offer cash prizes. In addition to money, these opportunities may help playwrights refine their craft and grow their resumes, professional relationships, and overall careers.

Royalties

If a playwright writes a commercially viable script that stands the test of time, she may receive somewhat regular, if modest, income through royalties. If she writes several such scripts, her body of work may begin to offer a greater, steadier cash-flow perhaps affording her more time to write.

Negotiation of royalties (including the percentage a playwright will receive, payment schedules, etc.) may differ based on various circumstances, most notably the party with whom the playwright is negotiating; this is generally a theatre (for non-published works) or a publisher. Other factors include the playwright's standing in the field, the source material (for adaptations), the resources of the theatre/publisher, etc. A playwright should consult with her agent or, if unrepresented, consult sources such as the *Stage Writer's Handbook*, Dramatist's Guild of America Business Affairs, or others listed in Appendix A.

Writing TYA vs. Youth Theatre

Some playwrights, acknowledging that it is difficult to make money in either TYA or Youth Theatre, may wonder if one route is more lucrative than the other. The answer to this question is entirely dependent on the playwright, the economy, competition, luck, and numerous factors outside the playwright's control; as such, there simply is no right answer to this question.

Per-performance royalties will usually (but not always) be higher for TYA productions than Youth Theatre productions. The individual contracts playwrights negotiate with theatres and/or publishers, however, along with their plays' appeal to producers (which does not necessarily correlate with quality), mean it is impossible to predict which of two high-quality scripts (one TYA, one Youth Theatre) would ultimately net the greatest profit.

Commissions

Playwrights can also earn money by being commissioned by a theatre to write a new play. Playwrights generally receive commissions only after they have proven themselves as both capable writers who can meet the aesthetic and practical needs of a given organization, and as people with whom it is easy to collaborate. When commissioned, the playwright is paid a negotiated amount (often including additional benefits such as travel and housing) that is based on the scope of the work to be done and the playwright's reputation. A well-established playwright is likely to earn a higher commission than an emerging professional, even if they are doing essentially the same work. Any TYA or Youth Theatre producer might offer commissions; however, the amount proffered is also determined by the available funding of the theatre or organization. In some cases, the sole remuneration may be a realized production of the script.

Grants, fellowships, and awards

Grants, fellowships, and awards that offer cash prizes (or workshops/productions) are also viable avenues for generating income and carving out time to write, as well as helping to further develop a playwright's reputation. Some grants and fellowships allot money specifically to provide playwrights time to concentrate on writing (either for a specific project or in general). Appendix D includes a list of selected young audience-related playwriting grants, fellowships, and awards. Playwrights should always remember to thoroughly check guidelines of any opportunity to which they may submit. There are certain opportunities in the general playwriting market that allow for the submission of young audience scripts and proposed projects, while others expressly state that they do not accept anything related to young audiences. That said, there are scripts that live in a crossover terrain (i.e., they could work for both adults *and* young audiences), so playwrights should check the organization's mission and use their own judgment.

***

In this chapter we explored some ways that playwrights might make ends meet while also creating time to concentrate on their craft. In our next chapter, we offer some concluding thoughts on why, given the inherent challenges (including the limited potential for monetary gain), people choose to work in TYA. Finally, we look toward the future.

Chapter 10

The Present and the Future

Over the course of this book we have explored many facets of theatre, playwriting, and how each intersects with young audiences. We first established that there is little agreement and much inconsistency in how TYA professionals (and indeed all of society) view childhood, adolescence, and infancy, what various terms mean, and of whom various groups are constituted. Similarly, we explored how "young audiences" is a malleable, often contested term. We explored commonly held misunderstandings regarding TYA. We discussed marginalization of the field and how this impacts those who work in it. We investigated the question of whether TYA is (or should be) a separate or sub-field of theatre, as well as disagreements over whether or not the writing process differs significantly from writing other types of theatre, and noted a unanimous sentiment among our respondents that TYA should not differ from other types of theatre in terms of sophistication and excellence.

We explored possible classifications under the TYA umbrella, such as by age-of-audience (e.g., TVY, teen audiences, family theatre) and by performer (e.g., TYA vs. Youth Theatre). We discussed ethical considerations including a playwright's need to be aware that all scripts are ideological, that the ethics of representation are complex, and that the field lacks consensus regarding who can tell what story. We broached the highly controversial topic of if and how issues deemed "taboo" or controversial should be introduced, and if so, how.

We discussed practical considerations concerning writing TYA scripts, such as how to access genuine child perspectives and the importance of playwrights being in touch with the TYA field as well as other artistic mediums available to young people on the wider consumer market. We explored the importance of avoiding assumptions about complexity of TYA scripts and the use of "advanced" language, as well as the debate regarding whether TYA should be educational. We investigated what playwrights should consider when writing for particular ages and forms of TYA (e.g., TVY, teens, musicals) and the needs of producers, including technical values, cast-size, and gender breakdown. We cautioned playwrights that adhering to these needs might not ensure production, so they should prioritize writing what they want to write over trying to please other entities. We explored adaptations in terms of business concerns and artistic approaches.

Next we explored the possible benefits of pursuing NPD experiences, the importance of previewing work before young audiences, and what it takes to be an effective collaborator. We discussed best practices regarding a script's process: write, produce, and then publish (or not), emphasizing that production should precede publishing. We presented a variety of perspectives from Artistic Directors about what they look for when choosing their seasons, illustrating that this can vary significantly based on the theatre's mission, aesthetic, and resources. We touched upon the importance of playwrights being active members of the field who create strong artistic and collaborative reputations. We noted that playwrights should continuously represent their work throughout their entire careers, as well as examined the pros and cons of getting an agent, while recognizing the potential difficulty in doing so. We pointed playwrights toward helpful resources for navigating the business side of playwriting and explored how to generate income (noting that this is often extremely difficult).

TYA is a complex, challenging, ever-evolving field that presents many difficulties to artists who choose to enter it. Regardless, many professionals do pursue this work, purposefully and with indefatigable energy. Given the sometimes intimidating, thankless, and frustrating nature of this field, we asked respondents why they choose to work in it. We include some of their inspiring and most varied answers below.

Why do you work in TYA?

Sandy Asher

"Because I enjoy the writing itself. Because I naturally tend to see situations from a young person's point of view. Because I love being part of this literary and artistic tradition. And because when it all comes together – the right script, the right company, the right audience, and the right venue – it's a high unlike any other. Whether that thrilling confluence happens with one of my plays or someone else's matters little. I'm hopelessly addicted."

Debbie Devine

"Because I want to persuade presenters to take chances, I want to persuade Equity to make a more reasonable touring contract so real quality artists can be sent on the road (not a single TYA Equity company is touring because it is cripplingly expensive for producers), and I want to persuade the sector to make deep, challenging, and a little bit dangerous art that matters. I can't lobby for these things without a great product."

Emily Freeman

"I work in TYA because of the challenges and the possibilities. It is said that structure or 'limitations' produce creativity. Knowing that I want to truly engage young people with my writing invites creativity. I love thinking critically about the entire theatre experience. How does the audience enter the space? How does the art shift the space, the audience members' emotional state, expectations, or how the audience views the world? What stays with the audience when they leave? I also write for this age group because of the potential for change. In my case, I am drawn to social justice stories, for example, And Then Came Tango, *which explores family diversity, sexuality, and love.*

In my experience, TYA that addresses social justice leads to unexpected outcomes. In my play, the story of two male penguins wanting to raise an egg of their own doesn't seem to alarm young audiences. Yet, adults and gatekeepers are launched into a reflective journey, questioning the subject matter's appropriateness, potential backlash, as well as their own identities, politics, values, and beliefs. The straightforward reaction from young audiences, the fact that they believe the two penguins should have a family, is a powerful catalyst for adult reflection and potentially even change. What a powerful and unexpected result!"

Jeff Frank

"I feel we have an inherent responsibility to make sure that a child's first theatrical experiences are transcendent – that they are witness to the power of theatre to touch hearts, stir emotion, provoke thought, and promote understanding and empathy. Great theatre can inspire change, and we are in dire need of change in this world of ours. I'd like to think that by producing theatre of the highest quality for young people and their families, we're not just developing future audiences, but actually developing the future of our communities."

Tamara Goldbogen

"I love the idea of creating what might be the first theatre piece that a young person experiences. It is this momentous responsibility to the young people in our audiences that helps me through every step of the production process – from script selection to post-performance opportunities. Personally, I find the family audiences to be the most challenging and I let that spur me toward producing the highest quality theatre that I can. If this is the only theatre that a child is going to see, then I want them to remember it for years to come and maybe, just maybe, this experience will lead them to seek out theatre in the future as an adult, for themselves or for their own children."

Barry Kornhauser

"There are many good arguments to be made for writing plays for young people, maybe even better ones than can be made for writing plays for their parents and grandparents. Firstly, while children enjoy art as much as anyone else, part of what growing up is all about satisfying a need to get in touch with the world. Theatre is an opening to do just that. Through our plays we can inspire young people to reflect upon the world they live in and even to explore ones they might otherwise never encounter. Our work can truly be transformative simply because our young audiences' lives are still taking shape. So in bringing them our plays, we are potentially opening gateways to new and diverse people, perspectives, and paths; fostering thought and sensitivity; evoking wonder and delight; igniting an imaginative spark; and helping share in the celebration of the human spirit. That is both a great privilege and a sacred trust. Aside from all this, children also happen to be very good audiences – unconventional, inquisitive, free of errant notions of what a play ought to be, and impeccably honest. What more could a playwright ask for?"

Joanna Kraus

"As a teen we performed on an outdoor traveling summer theatre stage. One day in a poor neighborhood, where many kids went barefoot, a little girl came up to me and presented me with a gorgeous red rose. I hesitated to inquire as to its origins. Instead, I asked, 'What's this?' She smiled shyly. 'You gave me something beautiful,' she held out the flower, 'so I wanted to give you something beautiful back.' That's why I write plays for young people!"

Jeremiah Neal

"I personally write TYA because theatre was such a strong influence on my young life. I found a way to express myself through writing that would allow me to watch the kinds of plays that I am interested in, and create the kinds of characters that I have seen develop in my own personal life."

John Newman

"Most of the playwrights who have chosen to commit their artistic lives to TYA tell me that they are drawn to the child perspective and TYA genre by instinct rather than by any pedagogical or political agenda. Many counselors would argue that all psychology is child psychology because the conflicts we resolve, or fail to resolve, in our youth will continue to confront us in adult life. Likewise, playwrights who define themselves in the TYA genre revisit childhood in their writing neither to escape into nostalgia nor to resolve trauma but to wrestle with the questions that they first confronted in their early years."

Tim Parati

"As a designer, I love the challenge of bridging the gap between the playwright's and director's visions and the children's imagination. It's our job, and joy, to interpret the playwright's thoughts into an actual scene that will make the children feel that they have stepped into the words. We frequently receive letters from kids who have seen our shows and it is comforting to see that if they have drawn a picture of the show, they often will draw what their imaginations have seen. For instance, they will draw the actual animals that the actors were playing instead of the actors in costume. They will draw a whole tree as opposed to the representation that we have created. Their minds fill in the blanks and that is beautiful."

Psalmayene 24

"My career path to writing plays for young people has been somewhat circuitous. Professionally, I've danced, acted, facilitated workshops, done music, and written plays for adults prior to writing plays for young people. It was not something I pursued, but rather something that pursued me. I believe in destiny, and I believe that we all have higher callings. Sometimes we follow the call, and sometimes we don't. I chose to listen and be pulled by the call of writing this type of work. And I'm happy that I did."

Roxanne Schroeder-Arce

"I don't seek writing for children; stories about children (and therefore often I guess for children) seek me. The audience is not in the forefront, rather the characters and their stories are. I do have a passion and mission to share underrepresented stories and serve underrepresented populations in my work."

Janet Stanford

"I produce and create for young people because this is my calling as an artist. I have come to think of TYA as a gymnasium for life. If a child goes with Jack as he climbs his beanstalk, outsmarts the wolf along with Red Riding Hood, and outgrows Neverland beside Wendy, she is flexing the mental and emotional muscles she'll need for the real world. As TYA artists, we have the privilege of making stories – old and new – that become a young person's reference points– their sources of strength, and inspiration – forever."

Hopes and dreams for the future

Looking forward, we asked respondents about their hopes and dreams for the future of TYA. These take many forms. Respondents wish to see an increasing pantheon of quality and innovative plays. They hope to work in a field in which practitioners are comfortable taking more risks. They long for a day when artists from all areas of the theatre – within and without TYA – respect work for young audiences. They crave increasingly diverse voices and stories. They share excitement about TVY's potential to inspire experimentation in all theatre and cultivate new audiences.

Some are excited about new models for play development/co-commissioning. Sandy Asher believes the field would benefit by adopting a model conceived by Tam Balmer in which three different theatre groups collaboratively commission a playwright to develop a new work. She notes that the groups decide:

1. What they need in a new script, in terms of topic, length, cast size, etc.
2. Which playwright they will contact about writing the script.
3. How much each theatre will contribute toward the commissioning fee and playwright's travel expenses.
4. When each theatre will produce the play and bring in the playwright.

Asher had the opportunity to work under this model and praised "the terrific cooperative spirit among the three groups. These three organizations were in the game for the development of a play worthy of their young casts and staged their productions in the best interests of the script's growth." In addition to the obvious financial benefits to all involved, Asher noted that this process was particularly beneficial because she "saw three casts who differed in age and experience; tested the script against production values that reflected budgets large, medium, and small; and revised with insights provided by professional, university, and youth theater experts" (Asher, "New Model" 32).

In addition to such models, we asked respondents about their own hopes and dreams for the future of TYA. They told us:

Olivia Aston Bosworth

"What I have found in researching other theatres producing TVY is they are interested in light and sound as a mode of storytelling. Many theatres that do not need to consider touring to local preschools and daycares have been creating incredibly imaginative spaces using very few words and more visual elements. The use of glowing objects, sustained sounds, and sweeping movement have been compelling audiences to fill in the blanks with their own experience.

Another trend I am very excited about is thoughtfully thinking of inclusivity. Theatres producing new works for young audiences are considering every kind of audience they could encounter, and are breaking down all kinds of barriers for these groups. Through non-traditional seating, smaller audience capacity for interactive performances, and the use of translators or imbedded foreign languages, theatres are becoming less of a place for people with money, and more of a community building space for all people of all abilities. At my theatre we are currently working toward this trend and finding new ways to engage families and early learners. My dream is for our Arts Center to become the weekend destination for children under ten years old. If they grow up in the theatre watching others communicate in various ways with diverse people, our new generation will be an inspired, empathetic, artistic youth ready to tackle all kinds of new developments in the world. I believe our future generations will be better equipped to be understanding of one another. This is the future I see, and I hope I'm a fortune-teller."

Michael J. Bobbitt

"I think that if we embrace our differences – a style, and galvanize all the parts of TYA, we would truly see that what we are doing is profound. Imagine what would happen if we celebrated the commercial successes of artists that occasionally create and produce TYA like Stephen Schwartz, Julie Taymor, and Rogers and Hammerstein. I suspect that shows like The Lion King are probably the most profitable theatre experiences of all time, seen by more people than any other one show. I also suspect that the creators of these shows would admit that they were creating shows for young audiences primarily – using specific skills and techniques to tell their stories."

Jeff Church

"I think we have a chance with the new Common Core teaching standards to gain some insight on what teachers could really use as a way to tie into their teaching in the classroom. I think there's a chance to move away from book adaptations being the driving decision,

because it's a real move toward writing about different sources on a topic, and much less about everyone in the classroom reading the same book. This is a real opportunity for us to do some commissioning around a topic or idea or theme. We've done a series of salons for educators in our area, and we learned a lot from these. I hope original plays can make a rebound!"

Melissa Cooper

"I hope the field continues to explore new approaches to storytelling, while also challenging our assumptions about what young people are interested in and what they can handle. I hope theatre can be a breath of fresh air for all its audiences, a place that celebrates life in all its complexity, contradictions, subtleties, dangers, and joys. For that, we need to embrace new forms and new content! I also hope some theatres will become less segregated in terms of age, allowing for multigenerational audiences. There are plenty of plays produced for teens or children that adults would love, just as young people need to see fine plays that were not written just for them."

Debbie Devine

"My hope is that playwrights see this audience as the hungry, thoughtful, and curious people they are and begin to write for their emotional and intellectual intelligence. It's important for playwrights to know that children don't have to understand everything. If they understand what's on the stage then they are being condescended to. We live in a sophisticated urban world where children are learning how to make their own entertainment digitally at two years old. We need to compete with that by telling marvelous relevant stories that make them ask questions and deliver the imagination that is the essence of theatre."

Jeff Frank

"As we look to the future of new plays in the TYA field, I think that we may start to see more community specific work. Four seasons ago we started our Wisconsin Cycle – a series of six new plays over six seasons that celebrate the rich heritage of our state. With these plays and associated workshops, special events and educational initiatives, we hope to celebrate the history and people of Wisconsin. These plays and their associated educational and community initiatives have engaged our audiences in a more powerful manner – opening eyes and deepening understanding of the stories and the people that comprise our community.

I remain concerned that with the continued ascent of technology we as producers of theatre may lose our way by chasing said technology and trying to corral it for use in our theatres. What we do best is to tell stories – stories of our shared human experience that ring true as they play out before our audiences. Let's hope we don't obfuscate the essential truths with spectacle, technology, and video. Often less is more. Give me a great story and some simple tools to tell that story, and I can craft a piece of theatre that invites audience members to be a part of the illusion. By evoking the world we are playing in rather than overloading an audience with detail and spectacle, we ask our audiences to engage with us, rather than to sit back and spectate. That is the kind of theatre I find captivating, and the kind of theatre I aspire to create."

Stephen Fredericks

"We are in the unique situation that we serve two masters in creating TYA. We have the target age the piece has been written for by the playwright and the adult that accompanies that child, is the teacher or school representative that booked it, or the patron that funded the project to begin with. By embracing the concept that you are not only charged with creating 'good' art as an artist, but also planting the seeds for appreciation for the arts in the future you share the responsibility and hopefully, open the door to collaboration with those that beforehand could only see the art as 'kiddie theatre.'"

Lauren Jost

"One of the reasons I love TVY is that it is so innovative – there is such a diversity of subject matter, performance style, venue, and audience. TVY is inherently multisensory, and I hope that it pulls TYA for older children in a similar direction. I love theatre that is visual, immediate, open-ended, and magical, and theatre for young children is at its best when it embraces the curiosity, innovation, and complexity of its audience. I hope that more companies choose to develop new work for very young audiences and deal with the complexities of producing work that is developmentally appropriate: small audience sizes, interactive elements, non-traditional staging and seating, family-friendly spaces. I hope to see a movement in the field that supports multisensory work that is small and intimate enough to be safe for very young children and children with special needs. We can't program this work into 500 seat houses, so we need to build new spaces and new funding models that can sustain equitable access to quality programming for children of all ages and abilities."

Michelle Kozlak

"I see scripts for young audiences playing with structure – finding new and creative ways to tell stories. Scripts are becoming more immersive, interactive, and inclusive – which I think is terrific. With TVY, we are continuing to explore what it means to create theatre for this young age group – what will those shows look like, sound like, and how will we continue to reach our audience in the future? Since TVY is still so new in the United States, continuing that exploration is very important."

David Wood

"A major development over the past few years is the embracing of theatre aimed at the under-fives. Such work hardly existed 20 years ago. Now there are many companies presenting plays specifically aimed at very young children. My own adaptation of Judith Kerr's The Tiger Who Came to Tea *is in its seventh year touring the UK, and has already*

played four West End seasons. I would never have dreamed this was possible when I began working in children's theatre and I find it very exciting that this kind of play is so much in demand. It is an extremely exciting and privileged experience being in a theatre full of children or young people who are responding positively, uncynically, with excitement and awe, to a play acted out live on the stage.

I would hope that in the future children's theatre will become even more accepted and acceptable in every theatre, and that any stigma attached to working in the field would simply disappear. Indeed it would be wonderful if the world would accept the fact that theatre for children is not the soft option! I would hope that writers and directors continue to come up with innovative productions, entertaining and serious, issue-based and story-adaptation. I would like to think, too, that the original craft of playwriting for children will be encouraged, rather than simply the adaptation of well-known books. And I would like to think that funding will continue to be found for our work, and, indeed, increased as the years go by, with the knowledge that exposure to the arts generally, and to theatre in particular, is a vital contribution to a child's education.

I cannot accept that theatre will come to be seen as old-fashioned and irrelevant. Only the other day I sat in an audience of children, all of whom have been brought up in a world of sophisticated graphic imagery on screens large and small. Onstage a shadow puppet elephant made its silhouetted appearance. It raised its trunk as a trumpeted sound effect played. The young audience gasped. Point made!"

Michelle Wright

"I feel that young people can be the most artistically challenging audiences to program for, and that is really exciting to me. The TVY section of our catalogue continues to grow, and the work being created there is so imaginative and free, yet has this underlying deep research and intellectualism. The duality is inspiring. Our field continues to figure out how we're bridging the gap between childhood and adulthood for teens in our theatres, and the work created for that group is so strange, and difficult, and wonderful. I would love to see more original work that reflects our diverse world, told by a varied array of playwrights. I also love the idea of having a kid-centric approach, where the young voices in these plays have been influenced by real kids."

***

We wrote this book because we dreamed that by exploring the challenges, risks, and rewards of this field and by drawing together the perspectives of many practitioners, we could begin to articulate the limitless possibilities inherent in TYA. We hope that our readers will add their voices to this vital conversation as it continues to evolve and unfold.

Appendix A: General Playwriting Resources

New playwrights seeking guidance on where they might begin the process of actually composing a play are fortunate to have many resources available. This book has primarily focused on issues specific to writing plays for young audience members. Many other books, however, offer writing exercises and activities designed to stimulate the writing process, descriptions of play development processes, and overviews of the field at large, including those resources that may help one to further navigate the business of playwriting. Fortunately, many activities and insights that are helpful in writing a play for general audiences are equally applicable in writing for young people.

This appendix includes texts new playwrights may find helpful, including those suggested by the artists we interviewed. Texts are listed alphabetically by author. This list is far from exhaustive, and we encourage playwrights to consult with bookstores and online retailers to locate additional texts they feel will best suit their particular needs.

Please note that the descriptions following each book are official descriptions from the publishers, rather than our own assessments of the text. The inclusion of any text here does not constitute our personal endorsement of that text.

Sources offering practical guidance on writing plays

Catron, Louis E. 2001. *The Elements of Playwriting.* **Long Grove, IL: Waveland.**

"With an infectious enthusiasm for the theater, Catron presents the basic principles of playwriting, including plot, dialogue, and character development, as well as the more complex issues of creating multi-dimensional characters and writing stageworthy plays that will attract producers, directors, actors, and audiences. Throughout, he sprinkles examples from classical and modern plays, provides exercises for sharpening and developing skills, and offers practical guidelines on working with actors and directors, getting produced and published, and finding an agent."

Dorf, Jonathan. 2005. *Young Playwrights 101: A Practical Guide for Young Playwrights and Those Who Teach Them.* **Los Angeles: YouthPlays Press.**

"A complete handbook for young playwrights and those who teach them, and for anyone who wants practical advice about the craft and business of playwriting."

The Dramatist

www.dramatistsguild.com/dramatistmagazine

"*The Dramatist* is the official journal of the Dramatists Guild of America, Inc. It is published bi-monthly and is the only national magazine devoted to the business and craft of writing for the theatre."

Jensen, Julie. 2007. *Playwriting: Brief and Brilliant.* **Hanover: Smith & Kraus.**

The author notes: "My favorite book on writing has always been Strunk and White's *Elements of Style*. They lay it out for you simply and directly, and they do not go on. You feel confident when you read that book; you don't feel overwhelmed or discouraged. So I've tried to do that same thing for playwriting. I've laid it all out for you without going on. I have just one suggestion before you begin. If you're inclined to write a play, you might want to read this book quickly, write your play, then read it again more carefully. [...] Tell the damn story. Then let this book help you fix it."

Sweet, Jeffery. 1999. *Dramatist's Toolkit: The Craft of the Working Playwright.* **Portsmouth, NH: Heinemann.**

"In *The Dramatist's Toolkit*, playwright and *Backstage* columnist Jeff Sweet offers an intensive and practical guide to being a working playwright. In this informative guide, Sweet discusses such matters as: the building blocks of playwriting; how characters relate to one another; the differences and similarities between musicals and plays; screenwriting vs. playwriting; and much more! Jeff Sweet offers guidance for the beginning playwright and advice for the seasoned professional."

Wood, David, and Janet Grant. 1999. *Theatre for Children: A Guide to Writing, Adapting, Directing, and Acting.* **Chicago: Ivan R. Dee.**

"Presenting theatre for children as a separate art form, [David] Wood draws upon his experiences as a magician, actor, director, producer, composer, and playwright, and analyzes the skills involved in entertaining and involving audiences of children everywhere. He reveals his special techniques for catching and holding a child's attention, provides a practical handbook illustrated with excerpts from his plays, and offers a behind-the-scenes look at the work that goes into them."

Zeder, Suzan, and Jim Hancock. 2005. *Spaces of Creation*. Portsmouth: Heinemann.

"*Spaces of Creation* [offers] insights, exercises and etudes intended to guide you through the process of accessing ideas and images from your own inner resources of mind and body. [...] They reinforce the depth and dimensionality of character by reconnecting you to your own child space, provide insights into plot structure through an examination of architectural space, and invite you to enter the dark territory of your dreams and your fears to release you from the phobias that inhibit creativity and risk taking."

Texts offering perspectives on new play development processes

Cohen, Edward M. 1988. *Working on a New Play: A Play Development Handbook for Actors, Directors, Designers, and Playwrights*. New York: Limelight Editions.

Theatre Journal describes this as "a groundbreaking book that explains play development to every participant in the process. It teaches the basics of the collaborative method that extends from the writer's first words through the opening night performance of the play, explaining how all the artists interact to combine everyone's visions into an accomplished, finished production."

Wright, Michael. 2005. *Playwriting at Work and Play: Developmental Programs and their Processes*. Portsmouth: Heinemann.

"In *Playwriting at Work and Play* Michael Wright [gives] you the ins and outs on eighteen major programs. Between Wright's discerning insight and interviews with program artistic directors you'll find the collective wisdom you need to determine how each of the eighteen might help you. In addition, Wright's discussions with professional playwrights, dramaturgs, directors, and other participants will show you how members of the industry view the work of play-development programs and how these programs impact the profession itself."

Resources related to legal and business matters

While this book is not intended to be a comprehensive exploration of the legal considerations and concerns involved in being a working playwright for young audiences, such issues and questions do arise. As such, we provide a short list of specific resources related to these matters below. Playwrights should conduct their own research based on their personal needs; in some circumstances it may be necessary for playwrights to seek the counsel of a professional attorney who is fluent in the legalese of the theatre and playwriting fields.

The descriptions of the resources below comes directly from their websites/publishers. Our inclusion of these resources here does not constitute our endorsement of these resources and shall in no way be construed as legal advice.

Dramatists Guild of America Business Affairs

www.dramatistsguild.com/businessaffairs

"The Guild's Department of Business Affairs is committed to educating members about business and legal standards in the theater industry while providing constructive comment to government and business leaders on balancing institutional tradition in the face of necessary innovation. Towards this end, the lawyers at the Guild draft positions reflecting Council's position on issues of national import, track US and worldwide theater business trends, and advise members on immediate business concerns." DG offers consultations, model contracts, sample clauses, term books, as well as access to Business Affairs article archives to dues paying members.

Grippo, Charles. 2013. *Business and Legal Forms for the Theatre, Second Edition.* New York: Allworth Press.

"Here is a complete, easy-to-use resource for anyone involved in the performing arts! This expanded edition contains 33 indispensable, hard-to-find contracts and forms that will save artists and performing groups thousands of dollars in lawyer's fees, while minimizing their legal risks. Attorney/producer/playwright Charles Grippo explains the proper use of each form in clear, concise language. No matter which side of the negotiating table you're on, you'll find plenty of practical advice to help you obtain the best possible deal. These ready-to-use forms and contracts cover every aspect of theater law, including author agreements, commissions, production license, play publishing, and more. Also included on a convenient CD-ROM, the forms can be copied electronically, modified, customized, and saved."

London, Todd, and Ben Penser. 2009. *Outrageous Fortune: The Life and Times of the New American Play.* New York: Theatre Development Fund.

"*Outrageous Fortune* examines the lives and livelihoods of American playwrights today and the realities of new play production from the perspective of both playwrights and not-for-profit theatres. The study, drawing on six years of comprehensive research, reveals a collaboration in crisis between the people who write plays and those who produce them. It represents the most comprehensive field study in the history of the not-for-profit theatre to analyze new play production practices and the economics and culture of playwriting in America."

Singer, Diana. 1996. *Stage Writers Handbook: A Complete Business Guide for Playwrights, Composers, Lyricists and Librettists*. New York: Theatre Communications Group.

"Written in a straightforward manner, with complicated matters clearly explained, *Stage Writer's Handbook* is truly a work no writer for the stage can afford to be without. Here, for the first time, Dana Singer gathers the information and ideas stage writers need to conduct their careers in a businesslike manner, with all the protections the law provides. Subjects covered include: copyright, collaboration, underlying rights, marketing and self-promotion, production contracts, representation (agents and lawyers), publishers and such developing areas as authorship, authors' relationships with directors, radio drama, videotaping and electronic rights."

Volunteer Lawyers for the Arts

www.vlany.org

"Volunteer Lawyers for the Arts (VLA) believes that individual artists and arts organizations deserve access to dedicated legal representation and advocacy to ensure that their voices are heard and that their interests are protected. VLA also believes that the arts community should understand certain legal and business matters to protect themselves and their work. To achieve these goals, VLA serves the arts community through 3 program areas: Legal Services; Education; and Advocacy. Our largest program, the VLA Legal Services Department, offers counseling and assistance to the entire arts community as well as our signature service of pro bono legal representation to low-income artists and nonprofit arts and cultural organizations. All of VLA's other programs are open to the entire creative community as well as the lawyers and law students VLA trains to serve the arts community […] VLA cannot assist artists with criminal matters, domestic relations matters, landlord-tenant matters unrelated to their art, business advice, [or] legal issues that do not have any connection to New York."

Appendix B: Organizations Serving the Field

Numerous national and international professional organizations operate to serve the needs of the field by advocating for theatre for young people; providing resources and professional development opportunities; hosting conferences, symposia, congresses, and festivals; and publishing scholarly and practitioner-oriented journals, magazines, and e-publications.

Below is a brief list (in alphabetical order) of some of the organizations actively working to promote playwriting for young people. This list is far from exhaustive; numerous other regional, state, national, and international organizations work to support the field. Playwrights should research what organizations best serve their individual needs.

While we do not include professional theatrical labor unions, advocacy groups, or other organizations that serve the broader field of theatre beyond TYA, it is important to note that they make invaluable contributions to the art form and can offer resources playwrights may find helpful. Such organizations include (but are not limited to) the Actors' Equity Association, Americans for the Arts, the Stage Directors and Choreographers Society, and the Theatre Communications Group. Likewise, many organizations dedicated to theatre and arts education (such as the Arts Education Partnership, EdTA, and the International Drama Educators Association) frequently address issues important to those working in TYA.

The descriptions following each organization's name are taken from their official websites. Inclusion in this appendix does not constitute our personal endorsement of any particular organization.

The American Alliance for Theatre & Education

www.aate.com

"AATE connects and inspires a growing collective of theatre artists, educators, and scholars committed to transforming young people and communities through the theatre arts."

AATE sponsors the following journals:

Incite/Insight

www.incite-insight.org

"*Incite/Insight* is an interactive online publication space for theatre artists, educators, theorists, practitioners, participants, critics, producers, administrators, and audiences to engage with the intersections of Theatre, Education, and Young People."

Youth Theatre Journal

Published by Routledge/Taylor & Francis Group

www.aate.com/default.asp?page=ytj

"The scholarly journal of AATE is a juried publication, dedicated to advancing the study and practice of theatre and drama with, for, and by people of all ages. It is concerned with all forms of scholarship of the highest quality that inform the fields of theatre for young audiences and drama/theatre education."

ASSITEJ International (The International Association of Theatre for Children & Young People)

www.assitej-international.org

"ASSITEJ proposes to unite theatres, organizations and individuals throughout the world dedicated to theatre for children and young people. ASSITEJ is dedicated to artistic, cultural political and educational efforts and no decision, action or statement of the Association shall be based on nationality, political conviction, cultural identity, ethnicity, or religion. ASSITEJ promotes international exchange of knowledge and practice in theatre in order to increase creative co-operation and to deepen mutual understanding between all persons involved in the performing arts for young audiences."

The Dramatists Guild

www.dramatistsguild.com

"The Dramatists Guild of America was established over eighty years ago, and is the only professional association which advances the interests of playwrights, composers, lyricists and librettists writing for the living stage. The Guild has over 6,000 members nationwide, from beginning writers to the most prominent authors represented on Broadway, Off-Broadway and in regional theaters."

doollee.com

www.doollee.com

"The free online guide to modern playwrights and theatre plays which have been written, adapted or translated, into English since the production of *Look Back in Anger* in 1956. doollee.com contains information on 50,364 Playwrights and 173,978 of their Plays."

International Performing Arts for Youth

www.ipayweb.org

IPAY services and supports "the professional community of performing arts for young audiences. Our membership is comprised of a growing worldwide network of artists, producers, presenters, agents, educators and students that are dedicated and involved in producing, presenting and promoting all forms of theatre, music, dance, circus, puppetry and more. We share best practices and industry resources, provide an annual community meeting place, and stimulate international dialogue and collaboration. IPAY is a bridge that brings together creative expression with business practicality, critical responsiveness and professional development."

National New Play Network

www.nnpn.org

"The National New Play Network is the country's alliance of nonprofit theaters that champions the development, production, and continued life of new plays. We strive to pioneer, implement, and disseminate ideas and programs that revolutionize the way theaters collaborate to support new plays and playwrights."

New Play Exchange

www.newplayexchange.org

A service of the National New Play Network: "The New Play Exchange is a streamlined script discovery and recommendation engine for the new play sector."

The Playwrights' Center

www.pwcenter.org

"The Playwrights' Center champions playwrights and new plays to build upon a living theater that demands new and innovative works."

Theatre for Young Audiences/USA (The United States Center of ASSITEJ)

www.assitej-usa.org

"TYA/USA is a national service organization whose mission is to promote the power of professional theatre for young audiences through excellence, collaboration and innovation across cultural and international boundaries. Founded in 1965 as ASSITEJ/USA, TYA/USA is the only theatre organization in the United States which has the development of professional theatre for young audiences and international exchange as its primary mandates."

TYA/USA publishes the following journal:

Theatre for Young Audiences Today

www.assitej-usa.org/tya-today

"TYA Today is a nationally and internationally respected magazine for the field of theatre for young people. Published semi-annually, *TYA Today* offers insightful articles about current issues affecting theatre professionals, editorials, and book reviews."

Write Local, Play Global (The Playwright's Network of ASSITEJ)

www.writelocalplayglobal.org

"An online meeting place for people interested in work written for young audiences. Think of it as a virtual café where you can read about, make contact and catch up with people from around the world. You can find out about exciting new work, how writers approach their craft and about organizations that support and develop the work of writers."

Appendix C: Recurring TYA New Play Development Opportunities

As discussed throughout this book, new plays can benefit greatly from the feedback of theatre professionals, young audience members, and others. Fortunately, there are NPD competitions, festivals, and symposia that take place on a regular basis throughout the United States. Below is an overview of some of these events in alphabetical order. While it includes some of the best-known development programs, the list is not exhaustive and playwrights should research additional opportunities. Additionally, because the dates, eligibility requirements, and submission guidelines for these opportunities may change at any time without notice, we strongly encourage playwrights to visit their websites before preparing any submission.

The descriptions below are taken directly from the websites of the organizations offering the programs; their inclusion here does not constitute our personal endorsement of any particular opportunity. We sometimes add notes regarding the frequency (usual time of year held, and submission requirements of some programs after the official descriptions) in italics.

New Plays for Young Audiences

Hosted by New York University at the Provincetown Playhouse (New York, NY)

steinhardt.nyu.edu/music/edtheatre/programs/summer/newplays

This program "honors the history of the Provincetown Playhouse where the early plays of Eugene O'Neill, Susan Glaspell, and Edna St. Vincent Millay were first presented. However, this series changes focus by devoting its efforts to development of new works for children, youth and family audiences written by both NYU students and noted authors in New York City, the US, and abroad."

The program is usually conducted annually with submissions due in the Fall.

New Visions/New Voices

Hosted by the John F. Kennedy Center for the Performing Arts (Washington, DC)

www.kennedy-center.org/education/nvnv

This opportunity "is a week-long biennial program for playwrights and theaters to stimulate and support the creation of new plays and musicals for young audiences and families. While at the Kennedy Center, selected playwrights, directors, music directors, composers, and actors work collaboratively in a weeklong intensive to further develop new works. After revisions, rewrites, and rehearsals of the new plays and musicals, the works are presented as rehearsed readings during a three-day conference for theater professionals, educators, and others interested in the field."

New Visions/New Voices is typically held in the spring of even-numbered years, with submissions due the previous summer (odd-numbered years). Playwrights must collaborate with a professional theatre company in order to submit their work.

Purple Crayon Players PLAYground Festival

Hosted by Northwestern University (Evanston, IL)

www.groups.northwestern.edu/purplecrayonplayers

This festival is a "nationally-recognized presentation of original, new work specifically for young audiences [that features] pieces by professional theatre artists and … works of Northwestern University students. The Festival [has grown] into a weeklong conference-style affair featuring workshops, guest speakers, development seminars for our directors, playwrights, and actors, and other unique events that span the Chicago and Evanston communities."

Ronald M. Ruble New Play Festival

Hosted by the Caryl Crane Youth Theatre at Bowling Green State University

www.firelands.bgsu.edu/arts/caryl-crane-youth-theatre

This annual festival showcases "new plays and musicals suitable for young adults and children" and seeks "the best and most promising unproduced theatrical works relevant to youth today. The weekend long festival, held at the beginning of May each year, consists of 3–5 staged readings of previously unseen theatrical works and will take place in the McBride Auditorium on the BGSU Firelands campus in Huron, OH. A winning work will be chosen through committee/audience/participant voting and the author(s) will receive a $500 prize as well as the option of a 3-week workshop of their production during the following CCYT season."

Write Now (formerly the Bonderman Playwriting for Youth Competition & Symposium)

Hosted by the Indiana Repertory Company (Indianapolis) and Childsplay (Tempe, AZ)

www.writenow.co

"Write Now is a national effort to advocate for playwrights and promote the development of new work for young audiences by: supporting the work of emerging and established playwrights through a biennial national competition and process-focused workshop; engaging a broad representation of the TYA field in an ongoing conversation about new play development; creating a stronger environment for new work by fostering connections and collaborations; and cultivating a common language of shared values about new work from the perspectives of playwrights, producers, community stakeholders, and academia." *Write Now is typically held in the spring of odd-numbered years. Playwrights who are US citizens may submit any non-musical script that has not had a professional production or been committed to publication for consideration.*

Appendix D: Grants, Fellowships, and Awards

This appendix includes several opportunities for recognition and funding that may be awarded to playwrights for young audiences. Many other opportunities can be located through sources such as the Dramatists Guild Resource Directory, the Playwrights Center, or the *Dramatists Sourcebook*, among other resources. We do not include below any opportunities that restrict eligibility (e.g., to entrants from particular geographic areas), so playwrights should be sure to look for additional opportunities in their state or region.

Many (though not all) general playwriting grants, fellowships, and awards specifically exclude plays for young audiences, so be sure to check the guidelines carefully before submitting to those opportunities. Also, while the opportunities listed below are open to TYA playwrights as of this book's publication, prospective entrants should check the website for each grant, fellowship, or award regularly as award amounts, entry guidelines, and other criteria may change without notice.

The award descriptions below are taken directly from the official websites of the awarding organizations; their inclusion here does not constitute our personal endorsement of any particular opportunity. Please note that while many of these opportunities are open to all playwrights free of charge, some have restrictions on who may enter and some charge entry fees. Be sure to check the website for each individual award.

AATE Distinguished Play Award

Sponsored by the AATE

www.aate.com/?page=awarddescrip2#Play

"Open to members or non-members of AATE, this award honors playwrights and publishers of the most outstanding plays for young people published during the past calendar year. The successful script should demonstrate superiority in execution, delineation of characters, theatricality, and appropriateness of style. Selected scripts should respect young people's understandings and abilities, providing them with perspectives on their own experiences while enhancing their imagination and emotional growth."

Aurand Harris Grants and Fellowships

Sponsored by the Children's Theatre Foundation of America

www.childrenstheatrefoundation.org/page3/index.html

These grants and fellowships "seek to inspire and challenge" TYA theatres and individual artists "to develop quality ideas and new opportunities in TYA, as well as promote live theatre experiences of high integrity for young people throughout the nation by supporting both individual theatre artists seeking to deepen and expand artistic capacities and opportunities through fellowship funding and by supporting TYA companies seeking to bring engaging live theatre to their respective communities."

Aurand Harris Playwriting Award

Sponsored by the New England Theatre Conference

www.netconline.org/aurand-harris-award

"This award was created in 1997 to honor the late Aurand Harris (1915–1996) for his lifetime dedication to all aspects of professional theatre for young audiences. A panel of judges named by the NETC Executive Board will administer this award. Two cash prizes will be awarded: First Prize of $1000, and Second Prize of $500. The judges may withhold prizes if in their opinion no play merits the award. A staged reading of the prize-winning scripts may be given, followed by critique and discussion."

Anna Zornio Memorial Children's Theatre Playwriting Award

Sponsored by the University of New Hampshire

www. cola.unh.edu/theatre-dance/program/anna-zornio-childrens-theatre-playwriting-award

This award is offered once every four years and "offers up to $500 plus [a] production for an unpublished play or musical for young audiences that has not been produced professionally. Plays, preferably with a single or unit set, should be not more than one hour long."

Beverly Hills Guild Marilyn Hall Award

Sponsored by the Beverly Hills Theatre Guild

www.beverlyhillstheaterguild.com/youth.html

"The Beverly Hills Theatre Guild annually sponsors the Competition for Youth Theatre to discover new theatrical works and to encourage established or emerging writers to create quality works for youth theatre. The Play Competition for Youth Theatre represents grades 6–8 and grades 9–12."

Charlotte B. Chorpenning Playwright Award

Sponsored by the AATE

www.aate.com/?page=awarddescrip2

"Open to members or non-members of AATE, this award honors a nationally known writer of outstanding plays for children, recognizing a body of work as opposed to a single play. It is named in honor of playwright Charlotte B. Chorpenning of the Goodman Theatre in Chicago."

Harold Oaks Award

Sponsored by TYA/USA

www.assitej-usa.org

"The purpose of the Harold Oaks/TYA/USA Honorees is to acknowledge the significant contributions of individuals and organizations in the Theatre for Young Audiences field in the US. Four to five organizations and/or individuals will be honored yearly at the annual TYA/USA membership meeting. We would like to honor groups in the following categories: professional theatres, arts organizations, publishers, college/university programs and individual artists and administrators in the field of young audiences. Nominees must be current TYA/USA members to qualify for the honor."

Jackie White Memorial National Children's Playwriting Contest

Sponsored by the Columbia Entertainment Company

www.cectheatre.org/playwriting.html

This contest "seeks to encourage playwrights to write quality plays for family audiences. Originally intended to find plays suitable for Theatre School production, the winning entries have been, and continue to be, produced for CEC's *Summer Family Theatre Program*, using actors of all ages."

KCACTF Theatre for Young Audiences Playwriting Award

Sponsored by the Kennedy Center American College Theatre Festival

www.kcactf.org/KCACTF.ORG_NATIONAL/TYA

This award honors an "outstanding KCACTF student-written play or adaptation on a theme for young people at any level between kindergarten and 12th grades."

Milken Playwriting Prize

Sponsored by the Milken Community High School

www.milkenschool.org/page/playprize

"The Milken Playwriting Prize is a theatre prize for plays that are written for teen actors to perform. The prize is $2,000, with a play development process culminating in a full production at Milken Community Schools. The goal is to encourage skilled playwrights and authors to write extraordinary plays that are suited to teen actors: shorter plays with large casts and more roles for females. Most playwrights today are focused on writing small cast shows for theatres, even though many opportunities exist for high school productions throughout the English-speaking world. The Milken Playwriting Prize winner will be widely publicized."

Orlin Corey Medallion Award

Sponsored by the Children's Theatre Foundation of America

www.childrenstheatrefoundation.org/page2/index.html

This award "honors recipients for their significant achievements for the enrichment of children in the United States and Canada through nurturing artistic work in theatre and the arts."

Princess Grace Awards Playwriting Fellowship

Sponsored by New Dramatists

www.newdramatists.org/princess-grace

"We encourage emerging playwrights to apply at the beginning of their careers so that through the New Dramatists Fellowship, they can develop their work as well as benefit from being a part of a unique, diverse, dynamic community of professional playwrights. An applicant's status as an emerging playwright is evaluated during the adjudication process."

Shubert Fendrich Memorial Playwriting Contest

Sponsored by Pioneer Drama Service

www.pioneerdrama.com/Playwrights/Contest.asp

"To encourage the development of quality theatrical materials for the educational, community and children's theatre markets, Pioneer Drama Service is proud to sponsor the annual Shubert Fendrich Memorial Playwriting Contest. This is an ongoing contest, with a winner selected by June 1 each year from all eligible submissions received the previous year. All eligible plays accepted for publication will be considered contest finalists, from which the winner will be selected. The contest winner will receive a $1,000 royalty advance in addition to publication."

The Pulitzer Prize for Drama

www.pulitzer.org/bycat/Drama

The Pulitzer Prizes have "honored excellence in journalism and the arts since 1917." (Note: to date, no play for young audiences has won this award; we encourage you to write the first one to do so.)

Tom Behm Award

Sponsored by the Southeastern Theatre Conference

www.setc.org/tom-behm-scholarship

This annual award provides $1,000 is "to an individual working or studying in the field of Theatre for Youth to seek professional development whether to attend a conference or assist with education credits. Individual also receives a one-year membership to SETC, registration to the SETC Teachers Institute and Annual Convention for the award year."

Theatre for Young Audiences National Playwriting Competition

Sponsored by the University of Central Missouri

www.ucmo.edu/theatre/about/write.cfm

This competition "encourages the writings of original works for children's theatre productions. [The 1st place winner] receives a $1000 cash award and World-Premiere production in the University of Central Missouri Department of Theatre's mainstage season. The production will receive six performances to potentially 2000 children and general audience members. The production will be entered as an associate or participating entry in the Kennedy Center American College Theatre Festival."

Appendix E: Select TYA Publishers and Producers

Publishers in the field

A number of publishers accept submissions of plays for young audiences. Some focus primarily on plays to be produced in youth theatre contexts (with young performers) and others on professional TYA. Some are large publishing houses that accept TYA submissions as part of a broader range of offerings. There are also companies that restrict publication opportunities to those who have produced their work with particular theatres or have other criteria preventing submissions from most playwrights; we do not include such publishers below.

The list below is not exhaustive and playwrights should conduct their own research into the company that is most appropriate for their play, as discussed in chapter seven. The descriptions of the companies below come directly from their official websites; their inclusion here does not constitute our personal endorsement.

Brooklyn Publishers

www.brookpub.com

"Brooklyn Publishers has been a strong source of comedy and dramatic plays for high school, middle school, and youth theatre for over a decade. Our reputation for powerful, well-written, yet easy-to-produce stage plays has grown each year. In addition to our many quality full length and one act plays, we offer the largest selection of ten minute plays and theatre books on the market. Our plays have won countless contests and awards and have been recognized for their dynamic plot twists, multi-dimensional characters, and overall strong writing."

Dramatic Publishing

www.dramaticpublishing.com

"Publishing fine plays since 1885, Dramatic Publishing is committed to developing and serving the authors, artists and educators who comprise the world of theatre. We offer musicals, full-length and one-act plays and high-quality theatrical books suitable for high-school theatre, children's theatre, professional theatre and community theatre. Our catalog includes a full spectrum of plays for every cast size, skill level and audience representing classic works as well as contemporary comedies, dramas and musicals of distinction."

iTheatrics

www.itheatrics.com

iTheatrics's mission is "to ensure young people everywhere have access to quality musical theatre programs by: adapting Broadway musicals for performance by elementary, middle and high school students; building intuitive teaching resources that guarantee educators have a successful experience producing one of our shows; creating study guides and innovative educational programs for Broadway shows; creating new musicals for family audiences [...; and] constantly researching and developing the absolute best practices that allow educators to create successful, cost-effective and sustainable musical theater programs."

Pioneer Drama Service

www.pioneerdrama.com

"Pioneer Drama Service [is] a leading play publisher for schools and community and children's theatres. [...] Our reputation among writers mirrors what customers worldwide think of us: we're friendly and easily accessible, responsive to their requests and honorable in all our business dealings. [...] Pioneer Drama's values permeate every aspect of the business, creating long-term partnerships with teachers, directors and playwrights. We share your passion. Like you, we believe theatre transforms lives and builds community."

Playscripts, Inc.

www.playscripts.com

"Playscripts, Inc. is an independent publisher of new plays and musicals, established in 1998 by brothers and playwrights Doug and Jonathan Rand. Playscripts plays and musicals represent a great diversity of voices, styles, and stories, and have been enjoyed in over 100 countries. We license amateur and professional productions, publish standard acting editions, binder books, collections, and eScripts. Our commitment to innovation has made Playscripts an industry leader. Our marketing reach extends beyond traditional channels, and focuses on connecting new plays with audiences."

Samuel French

www.samuelfrench.com

"Samuel French is committed to not only respecting the history of the theatre, as well as its own place in that history, but also leading the industry with new technological advancements and cutting edge literature. Samuel French is the dramatic literature resource for the English-speaking theatrical community and the champion of emerging playwrights. Our core values add up to this one thing – Making Theatre Happen. We value and celebrate all of the Theatre Makers out there, and it is our goal to support our customers and authors in any way we can."

YouthPLAYS

www.youthplays.com

"YouthPLAYS is a publisher of award-winning professional dramatists and talented new discoveries. We license one-act and full-length plays and musicals, including works both for teen and pre-teen performers, as well as adult actors performing for young audiences. All of our plays are available digitally, and most of them are available as physical copies as well."

TYA producers

Hundreds of theatre companies, schools, and other producing entities throughout the United States produce TYA productions on either an exclusive basis or as part of broader seasons. As discussed in chapter seven, some professional theatres accept unsolicited script submissions while many do not; it is important to consult the policies of any given theatre before submitting material to them. Given the vast number of theatres involved with TYA, we cannot begin to list them here. An excellent resource for locating companies invested in TYA is the *Marquee,* a publication of TYA/USA, which in 2015 included over 100 organizations such as theatre companies and other producers. Note, however, that *Marquee* only includes theatres that are members of TYA/USA and is therefore not comprehensive; nor does inclusion in this publication constitute our endorsement of any particular producer or other organization.

Bibliography

Aldrich, Nancy. "Re: Playwriting For Youth Book – Questions." Message to the authors. 24 Sep. 2014. Email.

Allen, Janet. "Re: Playwriting for Youth Book – Questions." Message to the authors. 11 Aug. 2014. Email.

Alrutz, Megan. "Re: Playwriting For Youth Book – Questions." Message to the authors. 06 Jul. 2014. Email.

Aries, Phillippe. *Centuries of Childhood: A Social History of Family Life*. New York: Vintage, 1962.

Asher, Sandy. "A New Model for Commissioning Plays: My Dream Experience." *Incite/Insight*, 3.2, 2011, pp. 32–32.

Asher, Sandy. "Re: Playwriting For Youth Book – Questions." Message to the authors. 09 Jun. 2014. Email.

ASSITEJ International. "Constitution." *ASSITEJ – International Association of Theatre for Children and Young People*. ASSITEJ International. May 2014. Web. 15 May 2015.

Bedard, Roger. "Negotiating Marginalization: TYA and the Schools." *Youth Theatre Journal*, 17.1, 2003, pp. 90–101.

Bedard, Roger. *Dramatic Literature for Children: A Century in Review*. Anchorage, KY: Anchorage Press, 2005.

Birner, William B., editor. *Twenty Plays for Young People: A Collection of Plays for Children*. Anchorage, KY: The Anchorage Press, 1967.

Bliznik, Sean, Rachel Hamilton, Margaret Hoppe, Craig Kosnik, Anne Negri, Aimee Reid, and Xanthia Angel Walker. "Working Between the Lines: Dramaturgy at the Bonderman." *Theatre for Young Audiences Today*, 23.2, 2009, pp. 10–12.

Bobbitt, Michael. "Re: Playwriting and Young Audiences Book." Message to the authors. 23 Mar. 2015. Email.

Bosworth Aston, Olivia. "Re: Playwriting and Young Audiences Book." Message to the authors. 21 Apr. 2015. Email.

Briley, Rachel. "Re: Playwriting and Young Audiences Book." Message to the authors. 20 Apr. 2015. Email.

Brooks, Laurie. *The Wrestling Season*. Woodstock, IL: Dramatic Publishing, 2000.

Brooks, Laurie. "Re: Playwriting for Youth Book." Message to the authors. 10 Jul. 2014. Email.

Brooks, Laurie. "Audience Engagement Beyond the Role of Spectator." n.d. TS. Courtesy of Laurie Brooks.

Buchanan, Matt. "Re: Playwriting for Youth Book – Questions." Message to the authors. 23 Jul. 2014. Email.

Burke, Adam. "Playwriting for Youth Book." Message to the authors. 8 Oct. 2014. Email.

Casas, José. "Re: Playwriting for Youth Book – Questions." Message to the authors. 02 Jul. 2014. Email.

Case, Sue-Ellen. *Theatre and Feminism*. New York: Routledge, 1988.

Chappell, Drew. "Re: Playwriting and Young Audiences Book." Message to the authors. 27 Mar. 2015. Email.

Church, Jeff. "Re: Playwriting for Youth Book." Message to the authors. 24 Aug. 2014. Email.

Clark, Beverly Lyon. *Kiddie Lit: The Cultural Construction of Children's Literature in America*. Baltimore: John Hopkins University Press, 2004.

Coleman, Maggie-Kate. "Re: Playwriting for Youth Book – Questions." Message to the authors. 10 Jul. 2014. Email.

Cooper, Melissa. *Antigone Now*. New York: Playscripts, 2005.

Cooper, Melissa. "Re: Playwriting and Young Audiences Book." Message to the authors. 28 Feb. 2015. Email.

Coulombe, Jeannine. "Re: Playwriting and Young Audiences Book." Message to the authors. 16 Apr. 2015. Email.

de Gelis, Stéphanie Félicité. *The Theatre of Education*. London: J. Wakater at Charing Cross, 1787.

Devine, Debbie. "Re: Playwriting for Youth Book – Questions." Message to the authors. 24 Jun. 2014. Email.

Dietz, Steven. *Still Life with Iris*. Woodstock, IL: Dramatic Publishing, 1998.

Dorf, Jonathan. "Re: Playwriting for Youth Book – Questions." Message to the authors. 06 Jul. 2014. Email.

Duffy, Peter. "Re: Playwriting and Young Audiences Book." Message to the authors. 15 Apr. 2015. Email.

Engelman, Liz. "Based on Trust: In Conversation with Linda Hartzell +Y York." *SDC Journal*, 4.2, 2014, pp. 23–27.

FastHorse, Larissa. "RE: Playwriting for Youth Book – Questions." Message to the authors. 27 Jul. 2014. Email.

FastHorse, Larissa. "Who Should Tell What Story, Amended." *tcg circle: beta*. Theatre Communications Group. 19 May 2014. Web. 15 May 2015.

Fendrich, Steven. "Re: Playwriting for Youth Book – Questions." Message to the authors. 10 Jun. 2014. Email.

Flood, Julia." Re: Playwriting and Young Audiences Book." Message to the authors. 26 Mar. 2015. Email.

Foon, Dennis. "Re: Playwriting for Youth Book – Questions." Message to the authors. 09 Jul. 2014. Email.

Frank, Jeff. "Re: Playwriting and Young Audiences Book." Message to the authors. 14 Apr. 2015. Email.

Fredericks, Stephen. "Re: Playwriting and Young Audiences Book." Message to the authors. 28 Apr. 2015. Email.

Freeman, Emily. "Re: Playwriting for Youth Book – Questions." Message to the authors. 08 Jul. 2014. Email.

Goldberg, Moses. *Children's Theatre: A Philosophy and a Method*. Englewood Cliffs, NJ: Prentice-Hall, 1974.

Goldberg, Moses. *TYA: Essays on the Theatre for Young Audiences*. Louisville, KY: Anchorage Press Plays, Inc., 2006.

Goldberg, Moses. "Re: Playwriting and Young Audiences Book." Message to the authors. 27 Mar. 2015. Email.

Goldbogen, Tamara. "Re: Playwriting and Young Audiences Book." Message to the authors. 15 Apr. 2015. Email.

González, José. "TYA Questions." Message to the authors. 25 Jun. 2014. Email.

Gregory, D.W. "Re: Playwriting For Youth Book – Questions." Message to the authors. 07 Jul. 2014. Email.

Gurman, Susan. "Re: Playwriting and Young Audiences Book." Message to the authors. 02 Apr. 2015. Email.

Hanlon, Tina. "Rex Stephenson's Responses." Message to the authors. 17 May 2015. Email.

Harmon, Nikki. "Re: Playwriting and Young Audiences Book." Message to the authors. 25 Mar. 2015. Email.

Hartford, Dwayne. "Re: Playwriting for Youth Book – Questions." Message to the authors. 14 Jun. 2014. Email.

Hepner, Murry. "Re: Playwriting and Young Audiences Book." Message to the authors. 02 Apr. 2015. Email.

Horton, Louise C. *Handbook for Children's Theatre Directors*. Cincinnati, OH: College Hill Station, 1949.

Hughes, Catherine, Anthony Jackson, and Jenny Kidd. "The Role of Theater in Museums and Historic Sites: Visitors, Audiences, and Learners." *International Handbook of Research in Arts Education,* edited by Liora Bresler. Dordrecht, Netherlands: Springer, 2007, pp. 679–699.

Ivey, Steven. "Re: Playwriting for Youth Book – Questions." Message to the authors. 03 Jun. 2014. Email.

Jenkin, Len. *Ramona Quimby*. Woodstock, IL: Dramatic, 1994.

Jennings, Coleman. *Six Plays for Children by Aurand Harris*. New Orleans: Anchorage Press, 1977.

Jennings, Coleman. *Plays Children Love*. Austin: Garden City, NY: Doubleday, 1981.

Jennings, Coleman. *Theatre for Young Audiences: Twenty Great Plays for Children*. New York: St. Martin's Press, 1998.

Jennings, Coleman. *Eight Plays for Children: The New Generation Play Project*. Austin: University of Texas Press, 1999.

Jensen, Amy. "Re: Playwriting For Youth Book – Questions." Message to the authors. 07 Jul. 2014. Email.

Jost, Lauren. "Re: Playwriting and Young Audiences Book." Message to the authors. 28 Apr. 2015. Email.

Kalke, Celise. "Re: Playwriting and Young Audiences Book." Message to the authors. 20 Apr. 2015. Email.

Kessleman, Wendy. *Maggie Magalita*. New York: Samuel French, 1987.

Kilpatrick, David. "Re: Playwriting for Youth Book – Questions." Message to the authors. 26 Jul. 2014. Email.

Koppera, Jenny Anne. "Re: Playwriting and Young Audiences Book." Message to the authors. 15 Apr. 2015. Email.

Kornhauser, Barry. *This is Not a Pipe Dream*. Anchorage, KY: Anchorage Press. 1993.

Kornhauser, Barry. "Re: Playwriting for Youth Book – Questions." Message to the authors. 27 Jul. 2014. Email.

Kovac, Kim Peter. "Re: Playwriting for Youth Book – Questions." Message to the authors. 23 Jul. 2014. Email.

Kozlak, Michelle. "Re: Playwriting and Young Audiences Book." Message to the authors. 30 Mar. 2015. Email.

Kremar, Marina. "Examining the Assumptions in Research on Children and Media." *The Routledge International Handbook of Children, Adolescents and Media*, edited by Dafna Lemish. New York: Routledge. 2015, pp. 39–45.

Kruckmeyer, Finegan. "The Taboo of Sadness." *Sydney Theatre Company Magazine*. 6 Aug. 2015.

Kruckmeyer, Finegan. "Re: Playwriting and Young Audiences Book." Message to the authors. 2 March 2016. Email.

Leahey, Kristin. "Re: Draft of Responses." Message to the authors. 21 Jul. 2014. Email.

Lee, Nick. *Childhood and Society: Growing Up in an Age of Uncertainty*. Philadelphia: Open University Press. 2001.

Lifton, Betty Jean, editor. *Contemporary Children's Theatre*. New York: Avon Books, 1974.

Lloyd, Mary Rose. "Re: Playwriting and Young Audiences Book." Message to the authors. 20 Apr. 2015. Email.

Ludwig, Jon. "Questions Playwriting for Youth." Message to the authors. 26 Jun. 2014. Email.

Lutwak, Mark. "RE: Playwriting for Youth Book." Message to the authors. 21 Jul. 2014. Email.

Macher, Samantha. "Re: Playwriting and Young Audiences Book." Message to the authors. 21 Apr. 2015. Email.

Manley, Andy. "Re: Playwriting and Young Audiences Book." Message to the authors. 15 Apr. 2015. Email.

Mason, Lorraine. *Beauty and the Beast: A Pantomime Story of Kindness, Beasliness, and Silliness*. Lazy Bee Scripts, n.d. Web. 15 May 2015.

Matetzschk-Campbell, Judy and John Newman. *Tell Your Story: The Plays and Playwriting of Sandra Fenichel Asher*. Woodstock, IL: Dramatic Publishing Company, 2010.

Matetzschk-Campbell, Judy. "Re: Playwriting for Youth Book – Questions." Message to the authors. 09 Jul. 2014. Email.

Menkin, Alan, Howard Ashman, Tim Rice, and Linda Woolverton. *Disney's Beauty and the Beast*. New York: Music Theatre International, 1993.

Mesner, Paul. "Re: Playwriting For Youth Book – Questions." Message to the authors. 22 Jul. 2014. Email.

Mitchell, Albert. "The Children's Theatre Audience." *Handbook for Children's Theatre Directors*. Louise C. Horton, editor Cincinnati, OH: College Hill Station, 1949, np.

Morgan, David. "Fwd. question response." Message to the authors. 29 Apr. 2015. Email.

Moses, Montrose. *Another Treasury of Plays for Children*. Boston: Little, Brown & Co., 1927.

Moss, Robert. "Re: Playwriting and Young Audiences Book." Message to the authors. 26 Mar. 2015. Email.

Murray, Beth. "Playwriting for Youth Book – Questions/Answers." Message to the authors. 28 Jul. 2014. Email.

Myers, Sarah. "Between Fiction and Non-Fiction: Performing Ethnography in TYA." *Theatre for Young Audiences Today*, 24.1, 2010, pp. 6–11.

Neal, Jeremiah. "Re: Playwriting for Youth Book – Questions." Message to the authors. 18 Sep. 2014. Email.

Negri, Anne. "Re: Playwriting for Youth Book – Questions." Message to the authors. 3 Jul. 2014. Email.

Newman, John. "Spotlight on Process: New Play Development at the Bonderman Youth Playwriting Symposium." Diss. New York University, 2006.

Newman, John. "Re: Playwriting for Youth Book – Questions." Message to the authors. 23 Jun. 2014. Email.

Oddey, Alison. *Devising Theatre: A Practical and Theoretical Handbook*. New York: Routledge, 1994.

Omasta, Matt. "The TYA Contract: A Social Contractarian Approach to Obligations between TYA Companies and their Constituents." *Youth Theatre Journal*, 23.3, 2009, pp. 103–115.

Omasta, Matt. "Adult Stakeholder Perspectives on Social Issues in Theatre for Young Audiences." *Youth Theatre Journal*, 29.1, 2015, pp. 73–86.

Omasta, Matt. "Survey of Stakeholder Perceptions." n.d. TS. Collection of Matt Omasta.

Parati, Tim. "Re: Playwriting for Youth Book – Questions." Message to the authors. 22 Jul. 2014. Email.

Pearson-Davis, Susan. *Wish in One Hand, Spit in the Other*. New Orleans, LA: Anchorage Press, 1990.

Pogrebin, Robin. "Broadway Babies." *The New York Times*. 30 May 2013. Web. 15 May 2015.

Portes, Elizabeth. "Re: Playwriting and Young Audiences Book." Message to the authors. 15 Apr. 2015. Email.

Price, Jonathan. "Re: Playwriting for Youth Book – Questions." Message to the authors. 30 Jun. 2014. Email.

Psalmayene 24. "Re: Playwriting for Youth Book – Questions." Message to the authors. 12 Jul. 2014. Email.

Rand, Jonathan. "Re: Playwriting for Youth Book – Questions." Message to the authors. 22 Jun. 2014. Email.

Revels, Jeffery M. "Re: Playwriting and Young Audiences Book." Message to the authors. 15 Apr. 2015. Email.

Romero, Greg. "Re: Playwriting for Youth – Questions." Message to the authors. 05 Jun. 2014. Email.

Saar, David. "Re: Playwriting for Youth Book – Questions." Message to the authors. 30 Jul. 2014. Email.

Saldaña, Johnny. *Ethnodrama: An Anthology of Reality Theatre*. Walnut Creek, CA: AltaMira Press, 2005.

Saldaña, Johnny. *Ethnotheatre: Research from Page to Stage*. Walnut Creek, CA: Left Coast Press, 2011.

Scholastic. 2015."Scholastic: Open a World of Possible." 2015. Web. 15 May 2015.

Schroeder-Arce, Roxanne. "Who Can Tell what Story?: Evolving Perspectives on Authenticity in Latino Theatre for Young Audiences." *Theatre for Young Audiences Today,* 22.1, 2008, pp. 4–8.

Schroeder-Arce, Roxanne. "Re: Playwriting for Youth Book – Questions." Message to the authors. 6 Jun. 2014. Email.

Smith, Marisa. *Seattle Children's Theatre: Six Plays for Young Audiences.* Lyme, NH: Smith and Kraus, 1997.

Stanford, Janet. "Re: Playwriting for Youth Book – Questions." Message to the authors. 12 Jun. 2014. Email.

Sterling, Pamela. *The Secret Garden.* Woodstock, IL: Dramatic, 1992.

Sterling, Pamela. "Re: Playwriting for Youth Book – Questions." Message to the authors. 25 Jul. 2014. Email.

Stevens Puppets. "Beauty and the Beast." 2015. Web. 15 May 2015.

Susman-Stillman, Amy. "Preface." *Igniting Wonder: Plays for Preschoolers.* Peter Brosius and Elissa Adams. Minneapolis: University of Minnesota Press, 2013.

Sutton, Mark. "For your book." Message to the authors. 5 Mar. 2015. Email.

United Nations. General Assembly. *Convention on the Rights of the Child.* 20 Nov. 1989. Web. 15 May 2015.

United Nations. General Assembly. *Resolution 50/81. World Programme of Action for Youth to the Year 2000 and Beyond.* 13 March 1996. Web. 15 May 2015.

van de Water, Manon. *Theatre, Youth, and Culture: A Critical and Historical Exploration.* New York: Palgrave, 2012.

van Kerckhove, Michael. 2014."The Adaptation Situation." *Theatre for Young Audiences Today,* 22.1, 2008, pp. 4–8.

Webb, Dorothy. "Response to questions." Message to the authors. 26 Jun. 2014. Email.

Wilhelms, Pat. "Re: Playwriting For Youth Book – Questions." Message to the authors. 21 Jul. 2014. Email.

Wood, David. "Re: Playwriting and Young Audiences Book." Message to the authors. 07 Apr. 2015. Email.

Woodson, Stephani Etheridge. "Constructing 'Children' and Creating 'Childhood' in the 1950s: Isabel Burger and Charlotte Chorpenning." *Youth Theatre Journal,* 14.1, 2000, pp. 132–143.

Woodson, Stephani Etheridge. "Re: Playwriting For Youth Book – Questions." Message to the authors. 17 Jun. 2014. Email.

Wright, Michelle. "Re: Playwriting for Youth Book – Questions." Message to the authors. 30 Jul. 2015. Email.

York, Y. "questions." Message to the authors. 04 Jun. 2014. Email.

Zacarías, Karen. "Crossing the Border: Writing for Adults and Kids." Write Local Play Global. 19 April 2011. *Write Local Play Global.* Web. 15 May 2015.

Zeder, Suzan. "Re: Playwriting for Youth Book – Questions." Message to the authors. 24 Jun. 2014. Email.

Notes on Contributors

The diverse contributors who share their wisdom, insights, and experience throughout this book are listed below along with their professional positions and affiliations at the time this book was prepared. We encourage readers to return to this list when they come across ideas from contributors they are unfamiliar with, in order to gain insight into the perspective from which the contributor wrote.

Nancy Aldrich, Artistic Director, Tears of Joy

Janet Allen, Artistic Director, Indiana Repertory Theatre

Megan Alrutz, Assistant Professor, University of Texas at Austin

Sandy Asher, Playwright, Pennsylvania

Olivia Aston Bosworth, Family Programs Manager, Alliance Theatre

Michael J. Bobbitt, Producing Artistic Director, Adventure Theatre MTC

Rachel Briley, Associate Professor, University of North Carolina at Greensboro

Laurie Brooks, Playwright, Flagstaff, AZ; Playwright in Residence, The Coterie Theatre

Matt Buchanan, Playwright and Composer, Massachusetts

Adam Burke, Artistic Director, Children's Theatre of Charlotte

José Casas, Playwright, California

Drew Chappell, Playwright and Faculty Member, Chapman University and California State University Fullerton

Jeff Church, Producing Artistic Director, The Coterie

Maggie-Kate Coleman, Playwright, Lyricist, and Librettist, New York

Melissa Cooper, Playwright, Writer, and Dramaturg, New York

Jeannine Coulombe, Manager of New Play Development, Stages Theatre Company

Debbie Devine, Artistic Director, 24th Street Theatre

Jonathan Dorf, Co-Founder, YouthPLAYS

Peter Duffy, Head of the MAT Program in Theatre Education, University of South Carolina

Larissa FastHorse, Playwright, California

Steven Fendrich, Publisher, Pioneer Drama Service

Julia Flood, Artistic Director, Metro Theater Company

Dennis Foon, Playwright, Novelist, and Screenwriter, British Columbia

Jeff Frank, Artistic Director, First Stage

Stephen Fredericks, Founder and Executive Director, The Growing Stage

Emily Freeman, Playwright and Community Engagement Director, Orlando Repertory Theatre

Moses Goldberg, Producing Director (retired), Stage One Family Theatre; Playwright and Freelance Director, North Carolina

Tamara Goldbogen, Beverley Taylor Sorenson Endowed Chair for Arts Learning, Weber State University

José Cruz González, Playwright and Professor, California State University, Los Angeles

D.W. Gregory, Playwright, Maryland

Susan Gurman, Theatrical Literary Agent, The Susan Gurman Agency, LLC

Nikki Harmon, Executive Director, Saving Endangered Species International Playwriting Prize

Dwayne Hartford, Associate Artist, Playwright-in-Residence, and Artistic Director Designate, Childsplay

Mireya (Murry) Hepner, Producer, MainStreet Theatre Company

Steven Ivey, Touring Manager/Core Artist, Children's Theatre of Charlotte

Amy Jensen, Dramaturg, New York

Lauren Jost, Artistic Director, Spellbound Theatre

Celise Kalke, Director of New Projects, Alliance Theatre

David Kilpatrick, Manager, Theater for Young Audiences, John F. Kennedy Center for the Performing Arts

Jenny Anne Koppera, Artistic Director, Spinning Dot Theatre

Barry Kornhauser, Playwright, Pennsylvania

Kim Peter Kovac, Producing Director, Theater for Young Audiences, John F. Kennedy Center for the Performing Arts

Michelle Kozlak, Producing Artistic Director, Arts on the Horizon

Joanna Kraus, Playwright/Author, California

Finegan Kruckemeyer, Playwright, Australia

Kristen Leahey, Literary Director, Seattle Repertory Theatre

Mary Rose Lloyd, Director of Artistic Programming, The New Victory Theater

Jon Ludwig, Artistic Director, Center for Puppetry Arts

Mark Lutwak, Freelance Director and Dramaturg, Seattle, WA; Former Artistic Director, Honolulu Theatre for Youth; Former Education Director, Cincinnati Playhouse

Samantha Macher, Playwright and Producer, District of Columbia

Andy Manley, Theatre Artist, United Kingdom

Judy Matetzschk-Campbell, Producing Artistic Director, Pollyanna Theatre Company

Paul J. Mesner, Artistic Director, Mesner Puppet Theatre

David Morgan, Artistic Director, Magik Theatre

Bob Moss, Freelance Director; Teaching fellow, Hollins University and Syracuse University

Beth Murray, Assistant Professor, University of North Carolina at Charlotte

Jeremiah Neal, Playwright, Nevada

Anne Negri, Playwright and Drama Specialist, Illinois

John Newman, Director, Noorda Theatre Center for Children and Youth at Utah Valley University

Tim Parati, Scenic Artist/Designer, Children's Theatre of Charlotte

Lisa Portes, Head of Directing and Artistic Director, Chicago Playworks, The Theatre School at DePaul

Jonathan Price, Composer, Playwright, and Director, California

Psalmayene 24, Playwright, District of Columbia

Jonathan Rand, Playwright, California

Jeffrey M. Revels, Artistic Director, Orlando Repertory Theatre

Greg Romero, Playwright, Montana

David Saar, Artistic Director, Childsplay

Roxanne Schroeder-Arce, Assistant Professor, University of Texas at Austin

Janet Stanford, Artistic Director, Imagination Stage

Rex Stephenson, Professor Emeritus of Drama, Ferrum College

Pam Sterling, Playwright and Associate Professor, Arizona State University

Mark Sutton, Associate Artistic Director, Children's Theatre of Charlotte

Dorothy Webb, Founder and Director, Waldo M. and Grace C. Bonderman Playwriting for Youth Competition and Symposium

Pat Wilhelms, Artistic Director, Roanoke Children's Theatre

David Wood, Playwright and Theatre Artist, United Kingdom
Stephani Etheridge Woodson, School of Film, Dance and Theatre, Arizona State University
Michelle Wright, General Manager, Plays for Young Audiences
Y York, Playwright, Washington
Suzan Zeder, Playwright, New Mexico

Index